SIGNPOSTS FOR HAPPY FAMILIES

Signposts For Happy Families

God, Your Marriage,
Your Family and You.

John Williams

JOHN RITCHIE LTD
CHRISTIAN PUBLICATIONS

40 Beansburn, Kilmarnock, Scotland

ISBN-13: 978 1 910513 21 7

Copyright © 2015 by John Ritchie Ltd.
40 Beansburn, Kilmarnock, Scotland

www.ritchiechristianmedia.co.uk

Typeset by John Ritchie Ltd., Kilmarnock
Printed by Bell & Bain Ltd., Glasgow

DEDICATION:
Gratefully dedicated to Audrey and our family:
God's special gifts to me.

Views expressed are not necessarily
shared by the Publisher

Contents

Preface

'Happy Families' was a simple card game children used to play. The idea was to see who could get a set of pictures of a complete family together first. It was fun as well as informative. Getting a real family together these days can be a challenge, but if we follow the right signposts, it can still be fun.

Signposts for Happy Families is written to help Christians and Christian leaders enjoy and share the blessings of marriage and family life, as designed for us by God. Now a signpost is a great help, providing no-one has turned it around! What's more, if we deliberately ignore it, choose the wrong road and get lost, it's no use blaming the signpost.

Unfortunately, today there are a lot of people who seem to think it's their mission in life either to turn around or destroy time-honoured moral and spiritual signposts. Indeed, the advice offered by some secular thinkers, sociologists and even many liberal theologians, is often so bizarre and contrary to common sense and traditional, biblical guidelines, that ordinary folk are asking, "Which way shall we turn?" or "Where have all the old signposts gone?"

That question reminds me of the situation we faced in England, in World War II. Because the government was concerned about the possible presence of enemy agents, as well as the threat of invasion, in their wisdom they decided to remove all signposts. That was alright for the locals who remembered their way around - even in the 'blackout'! But can you imagine the confusion of people who had to travel around the country on business? So, in our modern - or is it 'post-modern'? - world, we face the same dilemma, morally and spiritually.

Thank God, there still are unturned, reliable signposts to be found throughout the pages of the Bible. These are not always neat little sayings but down-to-earth, practical, proven principles of behaviour, discovered by careful reading of the inspired text. Hopefully that's where this little book will help. It is offered as a companion to the Bible, to assist in applying God's Living Word to real life situations. It is not intended to be a substitute for the services of a qualified, reliable, Christian counsellor, when one is needed. It is simply a guide book for husbands, wives, parents, singles, divorcees, teenagers and others, who are seeking to honour the Lord and follow His signposts. Remember, "You need never walk alone!"

Try praying the words of this beautiful old hymn.

"Teach me Thy way, O Lord, Teach me Thy way!
Thy gracious aid afford, Teach me Thy way!
Help me to walk aright; More by faith, less by sight;
Lead me with heav'nly light: Teach me Thy way!"
(B. Mansell Ramsey, 1849 – 1923).

Victoria, B.C., Canada - 2014.

Part 1

God's Gift of Marriage

"…holy matrimony: which is an honourable estate, instituted by God in the time of man's innocency, signifying unto us the mystical union that is betwixt Christ and his Church: …it was ordained for the procreation of children…for a remedy against sin… for mutual society, help and comfort."

(The form of Solemnization of Matrimony,
The Book of Common Prayer)

CHAPTER ONE

God's Blueprint

Marriage was instituted by God and is to be carefully cultivated and protected. It is both the purpose and fulfilment of our human sexuality and the proper context of family life and happiness. There are few more beautiful words about marriage than the following lines from the Book of Genesis:

"And the rib that the Lord God had taken from the man he made into a woman and brought her to the man. Then the man said, "This at last is bone of my bones and flesh of my flesh; she shall be called Woman, because she was taken out of Man." - Genesis 2:22,23.

In the Image of God

The Bible presents men and women as creations of God and interprets all human relationships in the light of that premise. As made in the image of God, we are personal, rational, responsible, creative, sovereign, spiritual beings. We are capable of moral choice and intelligent decisions; but also - and this is essential to marriage - capable of deep and meaningful relationships.

Of course, while as men and women we have these marvellous capabilities, at present we do not in ourselves have complete mastery of them, and thus are often frustrated. This is the result of what the Bible calls 'sin', and what theologians describe as 'human depravity'. Such a doctrine, despite its dire sound, does not lead to despair but to hope. However, it does cut us down to size and challenges us to turn in trusting obedience back to our

Creator. It is in this returning that we discover not only our full potential as humans but also new freedoms and new dimensions in our relationships with others.

'Man' as Male and Female

"When God created man, he made him in the likeness of God. Male and female he created them, and he blessed them and named them Man when they were created." - Genesis 5:1,2.

Usually, when we use the word 'man' we tend to limit it to the masculine gender. In the Genesis story, as for example in the verses cited above, the words 'man' or 'Adam' represent both genders. Maleness and femaleness are complementary expressions of the one whole that is 'mankind' as created in God's image. This in no way cancels out the reality that men are men and women are women!

This matter of human sexuality is important for our present study. Several things surface in the beautiful story told in Genesis 2:18-24. First, there is God's concern for Adam as a personal being. It is this, in the context of the story, which tells why God created Eve. Second, we see also the relational side of man. Adam as a personal being is seen as lonely and unfulfilled. He stands peerless in God's pristine creation but in need of a 'helpmeet'. If man is to realise his innate capability of relationship, he needs a "helper fit for him" - 2:18. This need is further evidence that man was created in God's image. The God of the Bible is not an impersonal, passionless, unrelated Being but a living Person who enjoys and expresses himself in intimate, personal relationships. - cf. John 1:1-2.

Third, we see the sovereignty of God in this story, as well as the response of Adam. God created Eve quite independently of man, but man immediately responded to her, seeing her as intrinsically herself and yet of himself. It is as though he looked in a mirror, liked what he saw and realised that the image was alive. As though he said, "She is me; yet she is not me!" This is even suggested in the Hebrew words for man and woman, 'Ish' and 'Ishah', respectively.

As we look more closely at this timeless story we learn a great deal about the basis of human relationships. It tells us that God 'built' Eve out of Adam. We read: "So the Lord God caused a deep sleep to fall upon the man, and while he slept took one of his ribs and closed up its place with flesh. And the rib that the Lord God had taken from the man he made into a woman and brought her to the man." - Genesis 2:21-22.

From the lovely imagery of this story we learn several things. First, man had nothing to do with the creation of woman. She was God's handiwork. It is almost as though the narrator is stressing this when he tells us that the man was asleep. Was this not simply a matter of anaesthesia but to make sure man did not interfere?

Second, while woman is independent of man, she is a part of him. Whether the writer intends us to think of a rib in the literal sense is unimportant. It is relationship that is in view. In any case, the Hebrew word for 'rib' may be read as 'side' (cf. NIV margin), which suggests that 'woman' is, in fact, one whole side of man's personality. There is a special beauty about femaleness. Yet this distinction is best understood when compared with maleness. Today many people tend to overemphasise and exploit the physical side of human sexuality. The Bible, while recognising this physical aspect, seems more concerned in the creation narrative to draw attention to the psychological and spiritual complementariness of a man and his wife in the plan of God.

It is sad, if not libellous, that in the controversy over sexism in our day, the Bible has been attacked and labelled as one of the supporting documents of male chauvinism. Misinformed women's liberationists have seen the Bible as the *magna carta* of male supremacy and have declared it off limits to all who want to establish women's rights. How unfortunate and how misinformed!

The truth is that no other body of literature has done more to establish the dignity of womanhood and to liberate her from repression and slavery than the Bible. The very Creation story we are looking at tells us why. It shows us that woman was created by God, not as a kind of toy for an imaginary 'macho Adam', but as his partner and friend. To use the insightful New Testament caption, Adam and Eve, as husband and wife, are described as, "heirs together of the grace of life" - 1 Peter 3:7 (KJV). Augustine, commenting on the Genesis story, suggested rather quaintly, yet pointedly, that God did not build woman out of man's head lest she dominate him; nor out of his foot lest he dominate her; but out of his side so that they would be partners.

Vive la difference!

Quite apart from men and women being psychologically and spiritually complementary, there is their physical diversity. This idea is clearly present in the rest of Scripture, as in the Genesis story. Sex is not a dirty word in the Bible but part of God's design and plan for the propagation and preservation of mankind (cf. Genesis 1:28). It has been well said that God performed the first marriage. As noted, the simple words of the Bible are, "...(God) brought her to the man." Perhaps Adam's heartfelt response was, "Wow!"

In the miracle of their heterosexuality, and the wonder of their mutual love, man and woman discovered both spiritual and physical fulfilment. Here lies the basic pattern for marital relationship. Anything different, be it a homosexual liaison, extramarital sex or polygamy, is an aberration according to Scripture, and is in fact under divine censure and judgment (Exodus 20:14; Deuteronomy 22:22; Leviticus 18:22; 20:13; Romans 1:24-27).

The procreation of children is a perfectly natural and expected result of marriage. Children, ideally, are born of an act of love which also satisfies human sexual desire. Here lies one of the bases of security within both marriage and family. This is part of the meaning of the words; "Therefore a man shall leave his father and his mother and hold fast ('cleave', KJV) to his wife, and they shall become one flesh" - Genesis 2:24.

Leaving and cleaving

Other important aspects of marriage and family are expressed in the words 'leaving' and 'cleaving'. They imply a unique and independent role for each generation and each new family unit. Once children reach adulthood it is natural and to be expected that they will leave their family nest and branch out to establish their own family and home. Each new family is not merely a surrogate group but a fresh, independent and responsible family under God. These words also imply a responsibility to understand that only as people properly 'leave' can they responsibly 'cleave'. This means that parents are responsible to prepare their offspring for marriage; and when marriage comes, to allow their parent-child ties to be loosed. It also suggests that the new couple, now joined together, must accept responsibility and conscientiously establish a new family unit. Young marrieds who feel threatened by 'severed apron strings' should understand that, while the 'cleaving' requires 'leaving', the 'cleaving' more than compensates for the 'leaving'! The word 'cleave' also suggests the permanence of the marriage relationship. More will be said of this later, but the Genesis story clearly implies monogamy, fidelity and permanence, at the very minimum.

Lost but not for ever

Something must be said about the effects of the 'Fall of Man', mentioned in Genesis. Whatever else was lost in the Fall, human sexuality survived. It was changed, and evidently bounded by new limits; but it was still a part of man the sinner. Some of the warmth of Adam and Eve's mutual trust must have evaporated after the Fall. Adam's laying the blame on Eve, for his own failure, would do nothing to increase her confidence in him, just as Eve's going along with the Tempter's suggestion must have eroded some of Adam's confidence in her (Genesis 3:10-13). Furthermore, subsequent to their disobedience to the stated will of God, they experienced guilt and fear. They also sensed a need to provide some covering for their nakedness. Not surprisingly, with the development of these new feelings of personal embarrassment, came an uneasiness in the presence of God whose fellowship they had formerly and regularly enjoyed.

Although Genesis tells us that God held our first parents accountable and punished them for their sin, it also shows us that he tempered his judgment with mercy. Divine punishment involved a number of things. For example, the pleasure of the procreative process was to be mingled with pain, just as the pleasure of work was to be blurred by toil. What is more, instead of the freedom and equality of Adam and Eve's spotless partnership, they came to know domination and subjection respectively. Man now reproduced in his own likeness and image (see Genesis 5:3). The image of God in man, though not obliterated, was badly defaced. Despite their failure and disobedience, God still cared for them. In the so-called *protevangelium* of Genesis 3:15, he even declared that they would still be his instruments in the ultimate plan of redemption and victory over evil. – cf. Hebrews 2:10-11 and Romans 8:22-23.

Without getting ahead of our story, how grateful we are to see the fulfilment of God's promise presented in the New Testament! There we see men and women redeemed by Christ and restored not only to relationship with God but also with each other. In Christ, man regains his liberty and a sense of dignity in work, while woman receives the promised blessing of God at childbirth (1 Timothy 2:15). It is in a truly Christian marriage, then, that we see the divine plan realised: the two "become one flesh" in the fullest sense.

In summary, to use a familiar idiom, "The battle may have been lost but the war would yet be won," – thanks to God's Grace! This is how Paul expresses it - "where sin increased, grace abounded all the more." - cf. Romans 5:20.

CHAPTER TWO

Points to Ponder

Seduced by Hollywood's lies and distorted lifestyles, and put off by the many failed relationships they see around them, today many young people have espoused a pessimistic, even warped view of marriage. Instead of seeking counsel or accepting proven, traditional Christian patterns, many are settling for all sorts of hopeless, sometimes weird experiments. These include 'living together', 'free love', 'common law arrangements', 'group marriage', 'partner swapping', 'trial marriage', 'same sex liaisons' – just to name a few!

Against this sad backdrop we are glad to be able to offer encouragement and say that there is no more wonderful experience on earth than a truly Christian marriage. We say this not simply as a matter of theory, but on the basis of life-long experience. Not only have we observed hundreds of happily married, fulfilled couples but, by God's grace, my wife and I have enjoyed over fifty years of a wonderful marriage relationship.

While it may be true that some marriages seem to be 'made in heaven' – and some elsewhere! – the fact of the matter is that the best ones are quite 'down to earth'! It's a bit like the old question, "Is life worth living?" The answer is, "It all depends on the liver," - in more ways than one! A good marriage is not caught – like the measles – it is the result of careful thought and loving consideration. Such a relationship may well be patterned on Paul's famous 'hymn to love' in 1 Corinthians 13. By the way, it's one thing to have that chapter read at your marriage ceremony; it's another to put it into practice afterwards.

Here are words from the marriage vows usually spoken before God and the congregation at a Christian wedding:

> "I take thee N. to be my wedded wife/husband, to have and to hold from this day forward, for better, for worse, for richer, for poorer, in sickness and in health, to love and to cherish, till death us do part, according to God's holy ordinance..."

These vows again remind us that marriage involves commitment, covenant and confidence in each other and in God. People who sidestep marriage, opting instead for living together, or whatever, generally lack all of the above. They also demonstrate a lack of will and an absence of trust. By saying that they want to "give it a try, before taking the marriage plunge," these people affirm their unwillingness to love without condition or reservation. They are tacitly assenting to the selfish concept that "if something – make that, *someone* – better turns up I can move on." Anyone party to such a precarious lifestyle is asking for all kinds of trouble and heartache. To voice the excuse that "it is better than a messy divorce," demonstrates a sad misunderstanding of human relationships, as well as a shallowness of character.

It goes without saying that anyone considering marriage should seek wise, professional counsel before taking such an important step. In fact, no minister or elder should agree to marry a couple until he has counselled them or guided them through a marriage preparation course. I remember having a conversation with a former Premier of the Canadian province where we live. While professing to be agnostic, he stated that in his view no government should issue a licence for marriage until the parties involved had successfully completed a marriage counselling course given either by a minister, a priest, a rabbi or a marriage officer. I think he was on to something!

Some Misconceptions

It is surprising how many people enter the 'united state' of wedlock starry-eyed, without a lot of thought and with a whole bunch of strange ideas: like the following:

"Love at first sight is the kind that lasts."

"An expensive, romantic honeymoon guarantees a happy marriage."

"We are going to update and rewrite those old-fashioned rules about marriage."

"We don't need any minister or counsellor interfering in our lives. We can make it on our own."

"If it doesn't work out we can always walk away."

"We must have a beautiful church wedding, preferably in one of those old village churches. It's not that we are religious or ever plan to darken the doors of a church again, but lots of other people do it and it makes for some lovely photo ops."

"Although we have problems and regularly quarrel, once we're married everything will be fine."

"There are some things I just can't stand about him but he will change." (That's the 'aisle, altar, hymn' approach!)

"Surely somebody that beautiful can't be all that dumb." (For a different slant, read Proverbs 11:22!)

"Although I am a Christian and my 'significant other' is not, I'm sure things will work out OK in the end."

We've heard lots of similar bright ideas. Our reply to each and every one of such musings must be: "Don't you believe it!"

Things worth keeping in mind

As we have discovered from the book of Genesis, marriage is an essential part of God's plan for the human race, not only for its preservation but for mankind's fulfilment and blessing. It is unfortunate that some elements of the Christian church teach that celibacy is of a higher order than marriage. Such a view is certainly not supported by Scripture nor, judging from current failure among many of the clergy, very sensible. Three things are worth noting at this point: First, God conducted the first marriage. Second, Jesus' first miracle in Cana took place at a wedding where he was a guest. Third, Paul tells us to forbid to marry is a mark of apostasy! (1 Timothy 4:1-3)

As Christians, if we have placed our life's decisions under the Lordship of Christ, then we can be thoroughly optimistic about marriage. Remember, God gave you to each other. You are therefore, as the Apostle Peter reminds us, "heirs together of the grace of life," – what a privilege that is! (cf. 1 Peter 3:7 KJV)

Characteristics of Christian Marriage

Scripture makes it abundantly clear that whatever strange ideas are proposed by our secular, contemporary society, the following should characterise a Christian marriage: commitment, faithfulness, permanence, responsibility, mutuality and, of course, love. Since we will give consideration to these marriage markers elsewhere in this book, we'll not expand on them further here. Although we mentioned this at the outset, it should be kept in mind that when we speak of a 'Christian marriage', we mean the union of a man and a woman who have both trusted in Christ as Saviour.

CHAPTER THREE

Jesus' Teaching about Marriage

While it is clear that Jesus set great store by marriage and offered clear, direct precepts about it, he did not teach a new view of marriage but reinforced the divine order in creation – see Matthew 19:4-6; cf. Genesis 1:27. In this chapter we will look at some of the important points Jesus makes.

The sexes complement each other

For Jesus, man is man and woman is woman, but neither is complete without the other as an expression of the Creator's purpose for the human race. In other words, heterosexuality is fundamental to our Lord's view of marriage. For him the difference of the sexes is what makes them complementary. This is basic to their roles in society as planned by God.

Jesus' teaching rejects the unisex philosophy of the liberationist as well as the unnaturalness of the homosexual. For Jesus, maleness and femaleness do not suggest conflict, strife and competitiveness, but harmony and wholeness. As we have noted, the two sexes teach us something about the nature of God.

The importance of monogamy

Our Lord's acceptance of the creation order is a clear statement concerning monogamy. He spoke of a relationship between one man and one woman: about "a man" and "his wife" becoming "one flesh." Then he added, "So they are no longer two but one flesh." There is not the slightest evidence that Jesus ever condoned polygamy. For him, as for Scripture as a whole, God's plan is one man for one woman (John 4:16-18).

Wherever we find polygamy tolerated or even practiced in Bible stories, we find spiritual declension and resultant problems. Only by the wildest stretch of imagination or by 'wresting Scripture', would anyone suggest that the Bible tolerates polygamy or bigamy. The fact that it recognises the existence of aberrations, and regulates their excesses, says nothing about God's condoning either.

Unity in marriage

By quoting the famous words, "Therefore a man shall leave his father and his mother and hold fast to his wife, and the two shall become one flesh," Jesus insisted on the oneness of husband and wife in the marriage bond. In case his hearers missed this, he adds, "What therefore God has joined together, let not man separate" (Matthew 19:6).

The Greek word translated 'hold fast', or 'cleave' (KJV), and quoted from the Septuagint Version of Genesis 2:24, comes from the verb *kollaō* which means literally 'to glue' or 'to cement'. In Matthew the verb is in the passive voice and reflexive mood thus further stressing the closeness of the bond. Obviously *kollaō* is used metaphorically here; but it is in the imagery of the word that we catch its true meaning. It suggests that just as two pieces of material once glued together cannot be separated without damage to each piece, so two people once joined in marriage cannot be separated without hurt to each one. Hence the wisdom of Jesus' injunction "let not man separate." His words have special meaning in this context, since not only is marriage being discussed, but also divorce. Jesus' point is that if we better understood the closeness of the *uniting*, we would better understand the tragedy and hurt of the *separating*.

There is no doubt that the unity mentioned here, "the two shall become one flesh," while including physical union, means something much deeper than that. It includes psychological bonding and, in the case of a Christian marriage, spiritual fulfilment. As a matter of fact, when a man and woman are united in marriage and live together in the fullness of that beautiful relationship, they seem to be fused into one, and sometimes even begin to think, act and even look alike!

The sanctity of marriage

Jesus' words, "what...God has joined together..." suggest further that marriage ideally is something arranged by God. Whatever else this implies, it says that marriage as an institution is sacred, and should be viewed as an inviolable contract. Jesus is reminding us that God, who performed the first wedding, in Eden, is still concerned about the success of every other marriage. In this sense there is a special sanctity about every true marriage. Let every bride and groom who seek true fulfilment and happiness remember this. If they in turn want God's blessing on their union, then let them seek God's direction and help before getting married. A marriage "in the Lord," to use Paul's phrase, is unbeatable (1 Corinthians 7:39).

The permanence of marriage

There can be no question that although Jesus dealt with the question of divorce in Matthew 19:9, he affirmed the idea of marriage as a permanent bond. His emphasis on the union in marriage, as well as his repeating the command for husband and wife to 'cleave together', make this plain. The further words, "What therefore God has joined together, let not man separate," are unequivocal.

Having looked all too briefly at Jesus' teaching about marriage, it becomes abundantly clear that he, in keeping with the rest of Scripture, held a high view of this unique human relationship. We shall be wise to heed his counsel and submit to his Lordship.

CHAPTER FOUR

The Apostle Paul talks to Husbands and Wives

The Apostle Paul's direct teaching about marriage occurs in five of his letters. They are 1 Corinthians, Ephesians, 1 and 2 Timothy and Titus. Like his Master before him, Paul based the validity of marriage on God's order in creation - cf. Ephesians 5:31. For him, marriage was not the result of man's social evolution or a matter of human convenience, but a gift from God. Whatever he taught about marriage was therefore conditioned by his belief in its divine origin. Whether he himself was ever married; whether he believed that some were called to a life of celibacy; or whether under certain circumstances Paul permitted divorce, are all incidental to his basic premise that marriage was instituted by God.

As we read what the Apostle has to say about marriage, it is important to recognise that he was not simply giving his personal opinion. He is certainly not offering what some call 'situational ethics' or 'culturally related, occasional advice', but writing under divine inspiration. This is clear not only from the tone of his writing but from explicit statements such as those found in 1 Corinthians 7:6, 12, 17, 35. We shall be well-advised, with the Apostle Peter, to read Paul's words as 'Scripture' - cf. 2 Peter 3:16.

The Apostle, like Jesus, believed in the sanctity of marriage; in its permanence, its exclusivity and in its beauty as reflecting the relationship between Christ and his Church. In stressing the importance of conjugal fidelity Paul everywhere commands purity and condemns immorality – cf. Romans 13:13; 1 Corinthians 5:1-13, 6:9-20; Galatians 5:19-21; Ephesians 5:3; 1 Thessalonians 4:3-8 and 1 Timothy 5:2. Significantly, he disqualifies from leadership in the churches any who are polygamous or inclined to entertain low moral standards - cf. 1 Timothy 3:2. As we look more closely at Paul's teaching we will focus on what he has to say particularly to husbands and wives.

The husband's responsibilities
He is a leader

Paul wrote: "But I would have you know, that the head of every man is Christ; and the head of the woman is the man; and the head of Christ is God." – 1 Corinthians 11:3 (KJV). This statement makes it quite clear, whether he likes it or not, that a Christian husband is called to be a godly leader in his home. He is not to be a dictator nor a despot, but a loving guide who accepts responsibility for the direction of his family. A Christian husband might well shrink from headship until he remembers that it is part of his obedience to Christ, his Head.

This acceptance of a responsible leadership role is important in the Christian home, as Paul's guidelines for elders and deacons show - cf. 1 Timothy 3. Not all Christian husbands are called to church leadership, but since all may desire this "noble task," the requirements apply to all men in the church. It is a challenging thought that how a man functions in his home has a bearing on his qualification for leadership in the local church.

Paul's teaching shows that the husband's headship has nothing to do with making valued judgments. The man is in no sense superior to his wife. This is clear from the apostle's reference to Christ's relationship to the Father. God is the head of Christ, not in the sense of being superior to him or prior to him, but in the sense that Christ accepts his role of Revealer and Redeemer, in submission to the Father. Remembering this, our roles are more easily accepted. Here is the Apostle's perspective: "For the husband is the head of the wife even as

Christ is the head of the church, his body, and is himself its Saviour." - Ephesians 5:23.

He is a lover

In the very context in which Paul talks about the husband's headship, he mentions the responsibility of the man to love his wife. Of course, there can be no true leadership in a home without love. Paul has much more to say about the husband's duty to love than about his duty to lead. He wrote: "Husbands, love your wives, as Christ loved the church and gave himself up for her, that he might sanctify her...In the same way, husbands should love their wives as their own bodies...let each one of you love his wife as himself." - Ephesians 5:25, 28, 33.

Paul's teaching is clear. The pattern for the husband's love for his wife is Christ's love for his Church. Just as Christ's love selected his heavenly bride; moved him to sacrifice himself for her, and leads him to be concerned for her present and eternal well-being, so a Christian husband is called to selflessly, even sacrificially, love his wife. Such standards are high, but we must remember Paul is talking about marriage "in the Lord."

A Christian husband's love will not be mere sentiment, but practical, considerate and kind. Writing to the Colossians, Paul urged, "Husbands, love your wives, and do not be harsh with them." - Colossians 3:19. The Apostle, speaking quite frankly, says: "The husband should give to his wife her conjugal rights, and likewise the wife to her husband. For the wife does not have authority over her own body, but the husband does. Likewise the husband does not have authority over his own body, but the wife does." - 1 Corinthians 7:3-4. He is pointing out that both the husband and the wife have duties to fulfil in the physical side of marriage. Neither must withhold sexual fulfilment from the other except for some mutually acceptable reason; and even then, only for a short time. The governing factor in all this would be love.

There are far more exhortations addressed to the husband to

love his wife than those addressed to the wife to love her husband. Paul is saying that a Christian husband must understand that his wife has a deep need to be loved and to feel secure in the expression of her husband's love. It is not difficult for a wife who is secure in her husband's love to submit to his leadership. She will feel neither threat to her womanhood nor any erosion of her spiritual authority as a fulfilled Christian wife.

He is a provider

Traditionally, and under normal circumstances, the husband has the role of 'breadwinner' or provider. He is called to care for his wife and family; to see that, as far as it lies in his power, they have a roof over their heads and food in the pantry. Paul speaks about 'nourishing' and 'cherishing' and the words he uses carry the sense of 'bringing up' and 'protecting from harm'. His point seems to be that, just as man naturally looks out for himself and cares for his own well-being, so he must have the same regard for his wife and family. Writing to Timothy, the apostle says: "If anyone does not provide for his relatives, and especially for members of his household, he has denied the faith and is worse than an unbeliever." – 1 Timothy 5:8.

Of course, there is much more to 'providing' than putting bread and butter on the table and milk in the fridge. As a matter of fact, these days, due to business mergers and economic downsizing, it is sometimes easier for a wife to find employment than for her husband to do so. This allows the husband to take on the role of caregiver for his family in a different fashion. He can become 'Mr Mum' as they say, spending time in more domestic pursuits and, in particular, looking after the children when they are small and still at home or in school.

There is nothing demeaning about a husband assuming this role. In fact, this can have great advantages, including opportunities for Dad to become bonded to his children in a very special way. He is thus still able to function as 'provider', with a difference. Rearing a family is demanding and ideally both parents are to share in it. Whatever income is available to the family is to be gratefully shared. Whoever 'brings home the bacon' is of secondary importance. The vital thing is togetherness. The one who goes out to work and the one who works at home are both doing the 'providing'.

The wife's responsibilities
She is a supporter
The Apostle writes: "[Submit] to one another out of reverence for Christ. Wives, submit to your own husbands, as to the Lord. For the husband is the head of the wife even as Christ is the head of the Church, his body, and is himself its Saviour. Now as the church submits to Christ, so also wives should submit in everything to their husbands." - Ephesians 5:21-24.

We may be tempted to write off Paul's words as "the teaching of a 'chauvinist bachelor'." However, to do so is to libel Paul who had a high regard for women and appreciated their ministry in the churches – read Romans chapter 16 and Philippians 4:1-3. Furthermore, it is to suggest that this part of Scripture, including its plain reference to Christ's relationship to his Church, lacks the imprimatur of the Holy Spirit – a desperate exegetical ploy indeed!

The Christian wife is called to submit to her husband's leadership just as both she and her husband are called to submit to Christ. This will not be difficult if, as noted, the husband leads according to the pattern set by Christ. In any case, Paul is not saying that the wife's submission is something the husband *demands*, but rather something the wife *gives*. What is required of the Christian husband and of the wife are both *gifts given*. One is loving concern and leadership; the other is support and submission. Incidentally, submission is a reflection of strength, not an evidence of weakness. There is no suggestion in Scripture that submission is in some way demeaning. It is the mark of the dignity of her Christian womanhood that a wife expresses her submission to the Lordship of Christ by accepting her husband's leadership.

One of the clever ploys of contemporary culture is to caricature a Christian wife's submission as subjugation. The truth remains that Christianity and the Bible have done more to emancipate women than anything else. Any system that teaches that a woman should not accept her husband's leadership role in the family is clearly not Christian.

Submission in the context of Christian marriage, of course, includes the wife's freedom to *make submissions*. A husband, who thinks he has all the answers or that the truth will die with him, obviously knows nothing about leadership and less about submission to Christ, his Head. By the same token, a wife who encourages her husband and refuses to denigrate him will reap great benefits.

Loving support will do more for a husband and for a marriage than will constant nagging and challenging his decisions. A wife will lose something of her importance and womanliness if she insists on 'wearing the trousers'. The dominating wife, by eroding her husband's leadership may very well lose the strong man she will one day need. It is also true that a domineering wife tends to raise disobedient offspring.

It will certainly help both husbands and wives to discover the blessings of a happy marriage relationship if they follow these words of Paul to the Colossians: "Put on then, as God's chosen ones, holy and beloved, compassionate hearts, kindness, humility, meekness, and patience, bearing with one another and, if one has a complaint against another, forgiving each other; as the Lord has forgiven you, so you also must forgive. And above all these put on love, which binds everything together in perfect harmony." - Colossians 3:12-14.

She is a homemaker
In his pastoral letters, Paul speaks about the importance of wives as homemakers. He writes: "They (the older women) are to teach what is good, and so train the young women to love

their husbands and children, to be self-controlled, pure, working at home, kind, and submissive to their own husbands, that the word of God may not be reviled." - Titus 2:3-5.

Women have a special gift for transforming a house into a home, and there is certainly nothing more desirable than a well-ordered Christian home. By the same token, there is no more noble calling than that of a wife and mother. How many godly, hospitable, contented wives and mothers have made deep and lasting impressions for good on their families, their church and society in general? If a woman feels frustrated by not being able to use her talents and training or to compete in the workaday world, today there are many opportunities for her to work from the home. There are also numerous church-related and volunteer service opportunities open to wives who have time on their hands. Thank God for the commitment and service of Christian wives and mothers!

A wife who is contented, kind, industrious, and hospitable is a blessing to any husband and family. She is worth her weight in gold – or rubies! - cf. Proverbs 31:10-31. Such a woman is unlikely to bring the Word of God into disrepute. It's worth repeating: Paul certainly appreciated the importance and value of Christian women, wives and mothers. - cf. 2 Timothy 1:5; Romans 16:13.

CHAPTER FIVE

'Occupational Hazards'

Marriage, like any other real life situation, presents its own 'occupational hazards' – to use modern jargon! Failure to recognise this or to ignore the wise, practical counsel of experienced guides is to court trouble. Too many couples head for the altar with precious little preparation and with even less awareness of the things that help make a marriage tick. It is foolish to think that we are clever enough to reinvent marriage or to suppose that we have all the answers.

This is not to suggest that marriage is 'all work and no play' - far from it! A good Christian marriage – and by that I do not simply mean a marriage between any two Christians, but rather a 'marriage in the Lord' – can be a little taste of heaven on earth. However, in this, as in any other relationship, a realistic approach is essential. After all, you cannot expect to fuse two disparate personalities into an intimate, life-long union that carries awesome responsibilities, without facing challenges. It is far better to be prepared, than to 'rush in where angels fear to tread', as the saying goes. Of course, angels don't marry anyway!

Most experienced counsellors will tell you that, generally speaking, there are half a dozen 'occupational hazards' facing married couples. They are: finances, in-laws, friends, sex, children and religion. Let's take a brief look at them and offer some practical tips.

Finances
This is one of the most common causes of marriage break-up.

Even though they may have discussed the subject briefly before their wedding day, many couples discover that once they face the nitty-gritty of budgets, business, bills and banking, finances can become quite threatening, if not overwhelming. One of the reasons for this is that different people have different ways of handling money. Some are impulsive spendthrifts – 'shop till I drop' types – while others are thrifty savers. Many young people have come to expect regular parental or social hand-outs. While the wiser ones have worked hard, saved and managed a personal chequing account, others think 'chequing' describes the pattern on his or her latest expensive shirt!

You can do a lot of things with money. You can save it, spend it, invest it, waste it or give it away. Of course, you can also worship it and become its slave. One thing you can't do is 'take it with you at the end'! Money is a tool and just like any other tool you can develop skills in its use, or wreck whatever you touch with it. It has a potential for good or evil. There is a saying - 'money talks'. One wag said, "That's true; as far as I'm concerned it always seems to say goodbye!" Because of our naturally acquisitive instinct - a modern euphemism for greed! - it is easy to develop wrong attitudes toward money.

The Bible itself recognises the potential of wealth for good or ill. Jesus warns, "You cannot serve God and money," and speaks of "the deceitfulness of riches." (Matthew 6:24; 13:22) He has an amusing comment about the rich man's attempt to enter heaven. He said that it would be easier for a camel to thread itself through the eye of a needle! (Matthew 19:24). Of course, some commentators try to help the rich man out – or is it the camel? – by explaining that the "eye of the needle" was a colloquialism for the small gate in an ancient city wall! In any case the lesson is: 'Unload whatever hinders progress'!

Jesus' parable about the 'shrewd manager' points to money's potential for blessing. It teaches us that we shall be wise to invest our wealth in soul-winning and missions, so that when we get to heaven there will be folk there ready to welcome and thank us for helping make it possible for them to be there. (Luke 16:9). Be sure to furnish heaven's 'welcoming committee' with something to say!

Paul writes to his friend Timothy, reminding him that "the love of money is a root of all kinds of evils" – not, as he is so frequently misquoted - "money is the root of all evil." - 1 Timothy 6:10. The Apostle goes on to tell Christians, whether newly married or well along the road, that they have a responsibility to contribute regularly, proportionately and generously to the Lord's work. The wisdom of such systematic giving, through our local church, is particularly apparent today, faced as we are with the shameless, 'tear-jerk begging' of some Christian agencies - cf. 1 Corinthians 16:1-2.

Against this backdrop, let's look at a dozen ways to make ends meet. Call it 'sailing out of the red sunset', if you will.

1. Decide to live within your means, at all costs.

2. Plan a budget; then stick with it! (See Appendix Three)

3. Avoid credit and unnecessary debt like the plague. Be especially wary of 'plastic money'. If you do use a credit card, discipline yourselves to pay your Visa or other bills by the due date! Of course, there is nothing wrong with taking out a proper mortgage, providing your desires are modest and the payments manageable. The same holds true for home and life insurance. In these, as in other mundane matters, let your head rule your heart, not vice-versa.

4. Do not fall for slick advertising that insists, "You can't live without our product" – almost certainly, you can!

5. Beware of thinking that you must have everything brand new. It's surprising how many *déjà vu* (i.e. used!) articles

are more durable than the latest ones, not to mention much cheaper! You can find all kinds of bargains at garage sales. Of course, avoid those places whose ads promise, "We buy junque and sell antiques," or "Genuine antiques made here!"

6. Do not expect to start where your parents are at. No doubt it's taken quite a few tough years for them to get there!

7. Avoid impulsive or compulsive buying. Some people are 'sitting ducks' for the fast-talking salesmen. They see – they want – they pay – they regret – they return – they complain – they are broke! It is always wise for couples to discuss and agree together before purchasing items, especially large ones, like furniture, appliances, the family car or even the family vacation (by the way, be sure to have one, even if it's in a tent!). Consult consumer magazines (at the local library!) and be sure to shop around. Look out for genuine sales and savings coupons. Remember, big brand names are not the ultimate criteria. Of course, beware of cheap 'Johnny come lately, fly by night' operations. It is still true - "You get what you pay for!" Of course it is also true that if you're not careful, "You get more than you bargained for!"

8. Neither partner should feel he nor she has the inalienable right to spend the family's money independently, particularly on the mistaken notion: "I earned it, so I spend it!" There is a sound biblical principle that reads, "For as his share is who goes down into the battle, so shall his share be who stays by the baggage (e.g. children and chattels). They shall share alike." (1 Samuel 30:24-25). 'I did it my way' is not a helpful theme song creating happy harmonies for married couples!

9. It is usually a good idea to decide amicably who actually handles the family finances (banking, bill-paying etc.). While 'many hands make light work', they can really mess up family money management. Here is a practical suggestion. Whoever

acts as family treasurer, it is best if it's someone who knows the value of money and who is open to advice. Here's a helpful hint, especially if one partner is required for one reason or another to be absent from the home for a while. Make sure the other one knows exactly where the bank is, where the important papers are, which bills need to be paid and when. Shun the impulse that says, "Go for it, there's no-one around to stop me!"

10. Most couples will find it best to keep a joint bank account (with a survivorship clause). Indeed, holding everything in common, including the family home, car and other valuables, makes for happier relationships and, in most circumstances, is sensible. Quite apart from making for good stewardship, it facilitates legal arrangements, particularly in the event of the decease of one of the partners. Of course, nowadays, due to the insecurity of many marriages and the sad divorce statistics, many couples draw up a marriage contract. There may be room for that sort of thing in some cases. However, this should not normally be necessary in a Christian marriage, where the Lord is recognised as the 'unseen partner'. Sharing and trust are the basic glues of any marriage. To insist on a 'this is mine and that is yours' approach cultivates independency, fosters family discord and undermines trust. Having said that, it is not a bad idea for each partner to have a small, personal 'fun money' account on the side. It acts as a sort of breather or safety valve and gives each person a sense of freedom.

Lots more could be written about family finances but much can be achieved through 'sanctified common sense', not to mention the helpful services of a reliable financial adviser. In any case, the time to begin family financial planning is today! Do you remember that rather pointed saying, "The road to Hell is paved with good intentions?" That's true not only of life but of finances too!

11. Above all else, cultivate the Christian grace of contentment - see Philippians 4:11-13; 1 Timothy 6:6 and

Hebrews 13:5. Here is a wise prayer from the Book of Proverbs: "…give me neither poverty nor riches; feed me with the food that is needful for me, lest I be full and deny you and say, "Who is the Lord?" or lest I be poor and steal and profane the name of my God." - Proverbs 30:8-9.

12. Although this may not come under the heading of 'finances', this will be a good place to mention that it is important to have a qualified person draw up your wills. People who die intestate leave a heap of trouble for their loved ones and make an unintended donation to the State coffers. By the way, making a will is a sign of responsible stewardship, not morbidity.

Family and Friends

The saying goes, "You can't choose your relations, but you can choose your friends." As far as newly married couples are concerned, relations and friends can be either a bane or a boon, hopefully the latter! However well intentioned, outsiders' comments and 'helpful suggestions' can create tensions, especially in a new marriage.

There are, of course, many true, as well as apocryphal stories about in-laws. Someone has said that behind every successful husband is a surprised mother-in-law! Fortunately that is not always true, but it does reflect a possible source of trouble. Fathers-in-law can be just as interfering, especially on behalf of their daughters. One unfortunate fellow said that he felt mixed emotions as he watched his mother-in-law drive his new Cadillac over a cliff! I must say, I had the best mother-in-law in the world. She would have done anything for our family, including me.

Parents naturally find it difficult to let go the reins of their offspring. They find it hard to understand why their own 'proven organisational genius' is not only unwanted but even resented! After all, they have provided and planned for Johnny's or Mary's life for years. It is hard to imagine that these children can make it on their own! What parents sometimes forget is that they themselves were young marrieds once, maybe even younger than the pair they are worrying about. Only recently I met a grandma who was telling her grandson that he was too young at twenty to get married. Bobby gently reminded grandma that she was only eighteen when she married grandpa - end of discussion!

There is also the danger of parents using money as a lever. Chances are the young couple haven't much of a bank balance – if they have one at all! – so father and mother offer help. That's all well and good and may in fact be necessary these days, but are there any strings attached? Do the well-meaning parents simply make purchases, even select a house or decide on furniture and décor – no questions asked – and expect the newlyweds to acquiesce? If not, do Mum and Dad get all upset, feel unappreciated and mumble about the possibility of funds drying up? That's the way it goes sometimes.

Here is a likely sequel to such intrusiveness. The young wife, or more likely the husband, resenting this kindly interference, gets upset and makes a few snide remarks about 'meddling in-laws'. To his surprise, his 'honey' dissolves into tears and comes to the rather vocal defence of Mum and Dad - "who were only trying to help us!" So now there is a deeper problem that will take some time to resolve. Incidentally, should such a situation arise, it is most helpful if 'wifey' speaks to her parents or 'hubby' to his. After all, blood is still thicker than water.

It is best, if at all possible, not to live with in-laws. Of course, in some societies, several generations live under the same roof. Furthermore, in some cultures, the older generations control decision making. In our shrinking 'global village', as younger people migrate, especially into western society, such ethnic traditions are challenged, if not abandoned. This creates further strains. Young people who opt to marry across racial lines will be wise to familiarise themselves with their future partner's family's social and cultural expectations, before taking the plunge.

Before moving on, one other matter will be worth noting here. People who come from large families have a totally different outlook on life from those who are 'only children' - just as do those who have been raised by a single parent or in a parentless situation. This is something to take into account; to discuss and deal with. An independent, self-motivated individual will not look at life through the same pink lens as the person who has always had their laundry done, not to mention their bed and lunch made for them. These sorts of things call for understanding, patience and a degree of compromise. Perhaps you heard about the couple who had to resolve a bedtime problem. This is the way the husband told it: "My wife didn't like to sleep in blankets; I didn't like to sleep in sheets; so we compromised, and slept in sheets!"

The Bible offers many practical guidelines for harmonious family relationships. One of them, already discussed, is this, "Therefore a man shall leave his father and his mother and hold fast to his wife..." - cf. Genesis 2:24; Matthew 19:5; Ephesians 5:31. Clearly the intent of this is that the newly married couple recognise that they have, to a greater or lesser degree, severed ties with their parents and established a new family unit. This is not to suggest there will be no on-going, meaningful, regular, happy relationship with Mum and Dad, quite the contrary. It is simply to point out the changed relationships, responsibilities, and security that come with the new family unit.

Now about friends: they too can sometimes cause problems. Most people have formed friendships before meeting their life's partner. Hopefully those friends will recognise they must now play second fiddle. If they do not, the young couple must make it clear that no friendship takes precedence over their marriage. They need to be especially careful about guarding confidences and intimacies and resist the temptation to discuss their spouse's faults and foibles with 'trusted friends'.

It can be quite disturbing when friends compare the virtues or vices of husbands or wives. Such odious comparisons can breed discontent and disillusionment. Not everyone hears or sees things the same way. It is a matter of keeping everything in perspective and recognising priorities.

Sex

In our sex-obsessed society it is important to develop a healthy, Christian perspective in this area of marital relationships. After all, sex is another of God's gifts to his children, which, like any other gift, can be cherished, enjoyed, indulged, or misused. Because of its potential for good or evil, it is vital for couples to talk together, both before and after their wedding day, about their physical relationship. Refusing to do so, for whatever reason, will generate all kinds of problems. All too often marriages fail and break down either through lack of understanding of our human sexuality, or through fear, embarrassment or lack of trust.

We do not intend to discuss the physiology of sex; this has been quite adequately dealt with elsewhere. In any case, this is best talked about by experts in the field, such as qualified Christian medical practitioners. A caveat here: ministers and religious leaders, especially unmarried ones, are usually ill-equipped to deal with this side of marriage counselling. Both they and their charges will be wise to recognise this! The following paragraphs are simply offered as quite general, practical guidelines.

1. Cultivate a wholesome attitude toward sex.

Unfortunately, many Christian couples come to their marriage with little true preparation for the enjoyment of their physical relationship. For various reasons, particularly upbringing or religious training – or, more likely, lack of both! – they are either thoroughly inhibited or unduly anxious to perform.

It is important to understand that physical love and sexual intimacy are thoroughly normal, and to be enjoyed, within the marriage bond. The Bible itself, while proscribing extra-marital sex, everywhere teaches that sex within marriage is natural and beautiful. Obviously, there is much more to marriage than sexual activity but without it couples not only lose out on a special dimension of human love but expose themselves to unnecessary temptations, frustrations and dangers.

2. While the physical intimacy of marriage is important, couples need to exercise mutual consideration. For example, a husband need not be over-demanding but respectful of the feelings and physical condition of his wife. By the same token, a wife need not be unduly withdrawn and reluctant.

As Paul suggests, "the wife does not have authority over her own body, but the husband does. Likewise the husband does not have authority over his own body, but the wife does." - 1 Corinthians 7:4. The Apostle goes on to recognise that while it is normal for couples to give themselves willingly to each other, there may be special times or circumstances when by mutual consent, couples temporarily refrain from sex. In passing, it is worth noting that Paul, writing under divine inspiration, offers the foregoing advice "as a concession, not a command" - cf. vs. 5-7. (The KJV reading here suggests that Paul is offering a personal rather than an inspired opinion. If we read him carefully, we shall see this is not what he means.)

3. While a good sexual relationship will do a lot to cement a marriage, a poor one will create problems. If problems arise in this area, then it is wise to face up to them and seek professional guidance. Seeking help is not a sign of weakness or failure but of wisdom and maturity. There are often physical or psychological factors that either inhibit or preclude a good physical relationship. Obviously, these are best dealt with sooner than later.

4. Sex should never be used as a weapon in marriage. To demand or withhold it with a view to 'getting what I want', or in order to punish a partner, is poor strategy and likely to backfire. Problems are best talked out before bedtime. Paul has another

piece of advice – applicable to singles as well as married couples – "Do not let the sun go down on your anger, and give no opportunity to the devil."- Ephesians 4:26-27.

5. Privacy and preparation will do much to enhance the special joy of physical intimacy. To rush into things without warm expressions of love and physical embrace is to short change each other and to miss much of the unique joy and wonder of this expression of human love.

6. Perhaps it goes without saying – we'll say it anyhow! – cleanliness and attention to personal hygiene encourage physical intimacy, just as much as a relaxed and loving attitude. Of course, cleanliness relates to the mind as well as the body. Beware of the insidious dangers and addictiveness of pornography and 'adult rated' TV shows and the like!

7. Discretion is particularly important. As noted earlier, to discuss your sex life with other than your partner – unless of course you are seeking professional help – is both unfair and unwise. As the writer to the Hebrews says: "Let marriage be held in honour among all, and let the marriage bed be undefiled, for God will judge the sexually immoral and adulterous." - Hebrews 13:4.

8. Different answers are given to the questions: "Should sex be engaged in only with a view to procreation?" "Should Christians use self-control or methods of contraception?" It would seem, in the light of both common sense and Scripture, that there is a need to exercise self-control, just as much in this special area of life as in any other. To engage in sexual intimacy with the attitude, "Well, if this produces offspring, so well and good; in any case that's up to God!"- appears to be both cavalier and selfish. It suggests that the law of cause and effect does not apply 'to us'! One wonders why any couple should think that they have an inalienable right to populate the already burdened planet Earth with their numerous offspring?

If sex for pleasure, within the marriage bond, is wrong, then it is hard to understand why God has given us such strong sexual drives, persisting even into old age. In the light of the words of Scripture – for example, Matthew 19:5, The Song of Songs, 1 Corinthians 7, and Hebrews 13 (quoted earlier) – it seems clear that within the accepted parameters of Christian marriage, morality and good sense, sexual pleasure is to be enjoyed.

Children

Having talked about the joys of intimacy in marriage, it seems natural to say something about children. After all, one of the purposes of the loving sexual relationship in marriage is procreation. This is the means by which the human race is naturally and normally preserved. Because of this it is essential that couples preparing for marriage, or those already married, give due thought and regard to this important topic. Children can bring great fulfilment and joy to a marriage; they can also cause division and heartache. We will expand on this in a later chapter. We touch on it here just to alert readers to the fact that children can sometimes be a challenge to a marriage. Young people will be well-advised to keep this in mind.

Religion

Here is another area of life that needs careful thought and understanding on the part of couples looking forward to marriage, as well as newlyweds. It is sometimes hard to think realistically about some subjects in the warm glow of a developing love relationship: religion being one such emotive subject. It is easy to say things like: "Well, we both believe in God; surely that's enough!" Answer: "No, it isn't!"

Often people grow up in the context of a particular ancestral faith. Parents, grandparents and other relations have inherited or espoused a set of religious beliefs that govern not only their personal lives, but their family ethics and social customs. In principle, there is nothing wrong with that. As Christians, we say that if our faith doesn't work out in daily living, in all its aspects, it isn't worth much! – cf. James 2:17.

The important thing is to face up to these facts early and make thoughtful decisions. It is too late, after the honeymoon, to discover that your partner either has no desire to talk about spiritual things or, on the other hand, expects everything to be controlled by his or her particular set of beliefs. The situation becomes even stickier if he or she demands that the children be reared "according to my family's faith," or insists that "no mention of anything religious will be made in front of the children!"

Speaking now more directly to Christian couples, it is absolutely vital to be united in the Lord. Surely, at the very least, a Christian who is contemplating marriage should determine only to marry a believer. As Scripture makes clear, there are some things that just don't mix and we shall be wise to heed its warnings. Be sure to read Paul's words in 2 Corinthians 6:14ff. In fact, it is not enough to marry a person simply on the basis that he or she professes to be a Christian. There are all kinds of other considerations and questions to be asked.

The Apostle Paul offers this basic, practical directive when writing about marriage: "only in the Lord."- 1 Corinthians 7:39. It is vital for Christians who wish to please the Lord and enjoy a truly blessed marriage, to seek God's will and obey it. They will discover that whatever issues arise, such as the upbringing and training of children, the conduct of affairs in the home, relationships with other people and society and so on, they are handled best by two people who, by mutual consent, submit to the Lordship of Christ.

Of course, other considerations come into play if, after marriage and the establishment of the family, one or other spouse becomes a Christian. This requires special grace and skill. Once again, the Bible is a valuable guide book. Nowhere, under such circumstances, is a Christian advised to sever a marriage bond because he or she, having come to faith, now finds himself or herself married to an unbeliever – just the opposite, in fact. Both Paul and Peter urge Christians to remain with their unbelieving partner, if at all possible. It is important to be patient and prayerful and to seek, not by preaching and pressure, but by gracious and godly example, to win over a loved one for Christ. See 1 Corinthians 7:12-13 and 1 Peter 3:1-7.

These then are some of the important matters to keep in mind if we would avoid what we are calling 'the occupational hazards of marriage'. Suffice to say, no situation or problem is beyond the grace and help of God.

CHAPTER SIX

What makes a Marriage Tick?

Having sounded the *Alert* we now sound the *All Clear* – so to speak. In this chapter we'll consider some of the most important keys to a successful and happy marriage.

Love

A marriage without love is like a day without sunshine. If two people marry from any other motive than true love they are missing life's best. That is not to say that a couple must always be 'kissing and cuddling'. It is simply to point out that love is the *sine qua non* of a good marriage relationship. True love is generous to a fault, self-sacrificing and concerned, first of all, with the well-being and happiness of its object. Love is not blind: it is most perceptive. The truth is, love chooses to close its eyes to faults and failure and loves without condition or price.

Love is not just an ephemeral, superficial emotion; it expresses itself in consistent action. It does this in two ways, in words and in deeds. The words of love must, of course, come from the heart and be sincere. To say, "I love you," just to make the big impression or get something you want, is unworthy mockery. But to say those three 'magic words' often and with feeling will do a lot for any marriage. Husbands need a special prod here. They, in particular, must beware of thinking that it is things that make a wife happy. A wife's primary want is to be loved and to be told so often!

Of course, actions still speak louder than words. While the "fruit of the Spirit is love," Paul reminds us that love has many facets or ways of expressing itself - cf. Galatians 5:22-23. Love is practical and can be expressed in little ways as well as big ones. Helping with household chores, sharing the care of the family, taking time to listen and sharing burdens are all important. Love will go to any lengths to accommodate and bless the loved one. On the importance of love over things, the writer of Proverbs declares: "Better is a little with the fear of the Lord than great treasure and trouble with it. Better is a dinner of herbs where love is than a fattened ox and hatred with it." (Proverbs 15:16-17)

Having said these things, let's remember that even if, until now, there has not been much love in your marriage or if you are partners in an arranged marriage - which of course is normal in some cultures - you can still 'learn to love' and discover the blessing of an enjoyable, close relationship. Love is much more than sentiment. If you will let him, God will revitalise your marriage. It may take time. Wise counsel will help. Be assured, the possibilities are endless. It will help greatly to read 1 Corinthians chapter thirteen together from time to time.

Optimism

Among the many beautiful thoughts about love, expressed in his famous poem, the Apostle writes:

"Love bears all things, believes all things, hopes all things, endures all things." - 1 Corinthians 13:7.

There's the nub of the matter: love is optimistic. While we might be put off by the contemporary, secular scene with its negativism about marriage and family, Christians can and need to be optimistic. Refuse to focus on your partner's weaknesses. Recognise and confirm his or her strengths. As the old song says: "Accentuate the positive; eliminate the negative!"

Of course it helps to look in the mirror before being too critical. For often it's a case of seeing 'our own faults writ large in others'. Keep in mind that a Christian marriage is like a golden triangle; a three-way partnership between two people and God! Someone has well said: "One person with God is a majority" – just imagine what 'two people with God' represents! Optimism involves time, thought and a commitment to hope, not just to 'play Pollyanna'. As noted earlier, a good marriage doesn't just happen, it's *made* by two people who believe in each other and who have made up their minds to succeed with God's help. A marriage is a bit like a beautiful garden: it is the result of patient cultivation and long-term care through all of life's changing seasons.

Communication

The key to any relationship, particularly marriage, is communication. Before their wedding day most couples seem to be able to communicate very well. They do it by words, looks, gestures and all sorts of other means. Furthermore, they seem to be able to talk about anything and everything – even 'sweet nothings' – for hours on end! I heard of a young couple who exchanged thirty minute tape recordings daily throughout their courtship. I hope they still find things to talk about. Wonder if they still listen to the tapes?

After the wedding day, as the months and years roll by, many couples fail to communicate. They do not appear to have the same enthusiasm for conversation. In fact, some husbands and wives can sit together evening after evening, barely exchanging a word. The television, the newspaper or a good book all too easily cut off their communication. We certainly need to be as aware of the danger of the 'telly' as of 'the sinister sound of silence'. A word of advice here, avoid using silence or sulking as a means of punishment. That can be most destructive and can fuel resentment.

I remember hearing an amusing story about an older couple who had always experienced communication problems. They had very little to say to each other apart from criticism. One day the husband went for his annual medical check-up. The doctor, amazed at his fitness and glowing tan, asked him his secret.

"Well, doctor," he said, "the minister who married us told me that if ever I felt like quarrelling with my wife, I should go out and do some work in the garden. To tell you the truth, Doc, I've spent most of my married life in our back yard."

Speaking of communication, be sure to say what you mean. If you're on the receiving end, listen carefully: make sure that you hear what is being said. By the way, *hearing* is not the same as *listening.* Communication is as much about listening as talking. Has anyone ever said to you, "You are not listening, my dear?" Don't forget about spiritual communication too. "Speaking the truth in love" and praying 'out loud' together are great tools for building a sound marriage. Of course, beside face to face communication, there are things like letters, emails and phone calls. When travel takes you away from home, keeping in touch is very important. It allays fears and says: "I'm thinking about you."

Considerateness
The Bible points out the importance of being considerate of other people and their feelings. For example, the Apostle Peter writes, "Likewise, husbands, live with your wives in an understanding way, showing honour..." (1 Peter 3:7; cf. James 3:17) Again, the writer to the Hebrews exhorts, "Let us consider how to stir up one another to love and good works." (Hebrews 10:24). Here's a useful exercise; get a Bible concordance and make a note of the "Let us consider" exhortations.

It is important to consider one another's feelings and susceptibilities, quite apart from material needs. A few sharp words spoken in anger or a sarcastic remark can cut deeply and take a long time to heal. It is especially wise to avoid putting your partner down in public, or contradicting them in front of friends or family.

We should also show consideration for a partner's physical needs. Sometimes, due to tiredness or poor health, a husband or wife may need a little extra 'TLC' (tender, loving care). A husband needs to be aware of his wife's emotional stresses, as well as her need to be loved and reassured. A wife will be wise not to 'dump everything' on her husband as soon as he arrives home 'bushed', after a busy day at work. Speaking of other needs, even Scripture itself advises couples to be sensitive to each other's physical needs - cf. 1 Corinthians 7:3-4.

In this context, let's say something about courtesy. The age of chivalry may be dead in some people's estimation, but not for a Christian gentleman. There is still a place for a gentleman to stand and assist his wife when she is to be seated at a table – not every last time, of course! And, however old-fashioned this may sound, a husband can still open the car door for his wife and treat her like a lady. Someone has said, "If you want your wife to treat you like a king, then treat her like a queen!" One jokester remarked, "If you see a man opening the car door for his wife, you can be sure that it's either a new wife or a new car." Surely not!

Appreciation

Here is another aspect of considerateness which is helpful in any relationship. We all naturally enjoy being recognised and appreciated. I've heard it suggested that "the highest compliment you can pay a person is to take him or her for granted." That is certainly not true in a marriage. To say "thank you" costs nothing but it pays good dividends in terms of a person's feelings and self-respect.

There are many ways of expressing appreciation in marriage. Here are just a few:

For husbands:
Thank your wife for taking time to prepare a nice meal.
Tell your wife that she looks great in that new dress (of course, make sure it is new!) and be sure to notice her latest 'hairdo'.
Take your 'honey' out for a special dinner occasionally.

How about a 'second honeymoon'?

A 'thank you' bouquet of her favourite flowers is important.

Breakfast in bed, now and then, will be very much appreciated.

How about encouraging the lady to take a day off every so often?

Of course, be sure to remember birthdays and anniversaries.

Here are a few 'don'ts':

Don't say how much better your mother's apple pie tasted.

Don't speak too appreciatively of other women's looks and clothes.

Don't wonder out loud why your friend's house always looks so much tidier "than ours."

Don't try to score points at your wife's expense, in public.

Don't share confidential secrets about your marital relationship, with your buddies.

Don't threaten or physically hurt your wife. I remember trying to counsel a young bridegroom who thought he had the right to 'spank' his wife! Can you believe it? I don't remember his coming to seek my advice a second time – I wonder why?

For wives:

Occasionally tell your husband that he really is a great guy.

Make yourself reasonably attractive (without monopolising the bathroom for an hour!).

Occasionally cook your husband's favourite dish.

Take time to encourage him, by being positive rather than negative.

Try not to be 'too tired' every night and morning.

Some don'ts:

Don't nag, or always put the blame on 'hubby'.

Don't tell him he's "hopelessly impractical."

Don't tell him his jokes are so corny or that you've "heard that one a hundred times before."

Don't keep telling him how kind and considerate your friend's husband is.

Honesty

'Honesty is the best policy' – that's never more true than in the relationship of husband and wife. Deceit and deviousness never pay. If you are at fault or have made a mistake, it never hurts to say, "I'm sorry!" Of course, honesty is just as important outside the home as inside it. Double standards undermine all relationships. It was said of one man that he was an angel at church but a devil at home. Such a man was plainly disqualified from Christian leadership, to say the very least. In this same vein, it is just as bad to take offence as to give it. Dealing with a problem openly and honestly can often defuse it.

A sense of humour

A sense of humour can be a real asset in a marriage. All sorts of difficulties can be resolved by a good laugh. We are so inclined to take ourselves too seriously. The Book of Proverbs - which, incidentally, offers a wealth of advice for couples as well as families, says, "A merry heart doeth good like medicine: but a broken spirit drieth the bones." - Proverbs 17:22 KJV. It goes without saying, of course, that vulgarity is not humour. Nor are 'funny stories' which are intended to demean your marriage or your partner's family. Remember too, teasing may sometimes be appropriate but it can be misunderstood and cause hurt. Good, clean fun is fine and is to be encouraged in all families.

Trust

Trust, in a marriage, is a two-way street. On the one side it is important not to give cause for distrust, on the other it is important to express trust and to resist the inclination to be unnecessarily suspicious. We need to trust each other just as much as we did the day we were married. But, above and beyond all else, we must learn to trust the Lord. He is more concerned than we could ever be about the success of our marriage and family.

Patience

In this day of 'instant dinners', 'instant puddings', 'instant coffee' and even 'instant porridge' (don't mention that in Scotland!), some people think in terms of 'instant marital bliss'! We are all inclined to be a little impatient; a bit like the man who prayed, "Lord, make me patient but please hurry up about it." Perhaps someone should have warned him that the Bible says, "…tribulation worketh patience." - Romans 5:3 KJV.

Cultivating a good marriage takes time and patience. After all, we come to our wedding day as adult people who have developed complex personalities with varied tastes, attitudes, ideas and desires. Obviously, welding two diverse people into a happy union requires forbearance and skill. Of course you need to be realistic. You are the same person after the wedding day as you were before it. You bring yourself to the marriage. Surprise! No alchemy suddenly changes you into Prince Charming or Sleeping Beauty.

We have to be willing to accommodate, to change our minds about some things and forget others. Some folk come to marriage with the 'concrete mind-set' – that is, 'thoroughly mixed and firmly set'! Clearly, things have to adjust and that calls for a lot of patience. Here's a tip, if your partner ever says to you, "You are so fussy!" – don't blow up, simply reply, "Aren't you glad, that's why I chose you!"

In marriage, as in other matters, if at first you don't succeed, keep trying! Difficulties and failures are often the means of character development for both partners. Remember, the end is worth the effort. The first few years are apparently the most challenging, evidenced by the fact that seven out of ten divorces take place in that period. The longer you go on, the deeper the roots of your love will grow, hopefully. Surprisingly, after the passage of time, 'those two different people' tend to become one in heart and mind. Believe it or not, as was suggested earlier, some couples even start to look alike!

Let Paul's words sum it all up for us:

"Love is patient and kind; love does not envy or boast; it is not arrogant or rude. It does not insist on its own way; it is not irritable or resentful; it does not rejoice at wrongdoing, but rejoices with the truth. Love bears all things, believes all things, hopes all things, endures all things. Love never ends."

1 Corinthians 13:4-8.

Part 2

Happy Families

"Your wife will be like a fruitful vine within your house; your children will be like olive shoots around your table. Behold, thus shall the man be blessed who fears the Lord. The Lord bless you from Zion! May you see the prosperity of Jerusalem all the days of your life! May you see your children's children!" Psalm 128:3-6.

CHAPTER SEVEN

Starting on a Family Tree

What is family?

"What a silly question!" you may say. "Everybody knows what a family is, don't they?" Well, I'm not sure, especially after being involved in a joint 'government and church' conference on the family! Today, for many people, particularly those on the fringe of society, the answer to that question – as to many others – is not that straightforward. Of course, I am aware that the word 'family' is used in all sorts of different ways today; perhaps that tends to cloud the issue. For example, we hear about 'the family of nations living in the global village'. Some people talk glibly about 'communal families', 'alternative lifestyle families', or even 'same-sex parent families'. Christians will sometimes speak of their 'church family'. And so it goes. Clearly in all these contexts 'family' is being used metaphorically, and rather loosely.

At the risk of being thought old-fashioned, in this book we shall look at family in a more traditional, time-honoured sense. We think of a family as a small group of individuals who are related to each other biologically and who often live together under the same roof. They are bound together by blood, by covenant, commitment and love. Such a family is capable of reproduction and continuance. Furthermore, since they share the same gene pool, family members often evidence similarities in appearance, disposition, personality traits and even in timbre of voice.

Nuclear and extended families

There are various ways of entering a family. Normally you are born into it, but you can also be married into it or adopted into it. The basic family, often called the nuclear family, is made up of Mum, Dad, Tommy and Mary. By contrast, the extended family includes siblings, grandparents, aunts, uncles, cousins, in-laws and outlaws! For those so inclined, an appreciation of the extended family will be reinforced by tracing out the family tree. These days there are all kinds of genealogy research agencies, some more authentic than others, who are willing to do the tracing for you. Be warned! Sometimes the more you pay, the better-looking your ancestral connections! Despite my own common name, one agency assured me that I had, among other illustrious forebears, no less a person than Oliver Cromwell. Of course they also suggested that I send my first instalment by cheque or credit card! Discretion being the better part of valour, I decided not to subscribe, though it might have been fun! I'll never know.

Other visions

While we are focusing on what we may call the 'genetic family', there are other relational communities that can be helpful. Such groups are especially helpful for people who for one reason or another, often through no fault of their own, find themselves isolated and with no known family connections.

The 'Surrogate Family'

This term describes a family which functions unofficially as a kind of adopting family. Perhaps parents or grandparents have left or died and children feel isolated and insecure. The surrogate family then assumes the role of kin and helps restore a sense of belonging. This is meaningful in our contemporary, mobile, often rootless society. Many churches have discovered this kind of thing can be very productive in establishing relationships and fellowship in their geographical community area. Organisations like 'Grandparents Anonymous' or 'Substitute Parents' can bring a new dimension of life to those they take care of. And, of course, this cuts both ways. Many lonely, older adults have found great fulfilment through their associations with young people.

Let me share a personal experience. I was a ten-year-old only child when my own mother died. Although my father was a wonderful friend to me and tried to make up for our loss, he had to carry on with his daily work and other responsibilities. It was then I discovered a very supportive network of 'aunts and uncles' who became my surrogate family. I shall always be grateful for their kindness and concern. Most of them were members of the little village chapel we attended. They put their faith into practice on my behalf.

'Buddy Families'

Another helpful system is one where families who are succeeding are willing to lend a hand to others who are not. By adopting a kind of 'buddy system' families can support each other. There are few families that have never known crises of one kind or another. Those who have survived and have found strength through the experience can encourage others who are going through tough times.

Obviously, this sort of thing calls for great skill and understanding. It is important not be intrusive, controlling or always on the phone. Such relationships call for great sensitivity, not to mention patience. Shared meals, outings and times together, within reason, can be encouraging. By the same token, too much of a good thing can be as bad as too little. The supporting family needs to avoid cultivating a co-dependency syndrome. Families, even dysfunctional ones, should be encouraged to stand on their own feet and accept responsibility, as much as possible.

Are you ready for family?

Having talked generally about 'family', let's look at some more real family situations and consider a few down to earth questions. Here are a couple of starters - "Shall we or shall we not have children? If so, then how many?" Those are pretty basic questions, at least as far as starting on a family tree is concerned.

Some people come to marriage with a great desire for family. This may be the result of their own early family experiences, either good or bad. People who have grown up in ideal family situations may want to pass their happiness on to others. Others who have had traumatic, sad early childhood experiences may determine to break such a cycle and set up a home full of the laughter and joy of family. Of course, some may take a much more negative view.

Whatever our background and however we may have been predisposed to having or not having family, it is important to recognise that while children bring their joys and sorrows they also bring tremendous responsibilities. To forget this and to start on a family tree with little or no consideration for the consequences is to court disaster for both parents and children. Couples need to be in agreement about wanting children and how many. Hopefully the following questions and comments will stimulate our thinking and help prepare us for one of life's great experiences.

1. Do we truly value life as a wonderful gift from God? As Christians, are we unreservedly committed to the belief that we are "heirs together of the grace of life" – to come back again to the Apostle Peter's beautiful phrase? (1 Peter 3:7 KJV).

2. Are we ready to accept the fact that to have children means being willing to share and sacrifice – not just money – but love, time, sleep, space, leisure and patience, among other things? Since children require constant care, feeding, nurturing, discipline, guidance and love, are we ready to welcome them with open arms? Are we ready to set aside our own ambitions and aspirations, even if only temporarily?

3. Do we really understand that raising children is a demanding, full-time job, especially when they are young?

4. Have we carefully considered our motives for wanting or

not wanting a family? That may sound like a strange question in our contemporary scene but it is important. In earlier times, particularly in agrarian societies, children were practically essential for family survival. They were needed to assist on the farm, to protect the family interests and to care for their aging parents. And, of course, due to short life expectancy, not all the children were likely to reach adulthood, so large families offered a kind of survival insurance. Much of what the Bible says about family is set in this social context. Here, for example, are words from a Psalm usually attributed to Solomon:

"Behold, children are a heritage from the Lord, the fruit of the womb a reward. Like arrows in the hand of a warrior are the children of one's youth. Blessed is the man who fills his quiver with them! He shall not be put to shame when he speaks with his enemies in the gate." - Psalm 127:3-5.

Today, in our western society with its built-in social shelters, the need for children as a means of family survival is not the same. However, there may well be other dangers thanks to 'social hand-out programs'. People may procreate thoughtlessly. They know they can milk the system, produce numerous progeny and then count on being subsidised from the public purse. Their motto seems to run: "Have fun! Why work? Let the government do it for us!" Now, since we are writing for Christian families, hopefully such attitudes do not obtain. Of course, there may be other questionable motives too. For example, some people want a large family because they regard that as a kind of status symbol or as a means of 'keeping up with the Joneses'. Yet others seem to think that a large family is inevitable if you are going to enjoy a full sexual relationship. Their attitude is, "Let 'em all come: it's God's fault, not ours, if we procreate!" Self-control and common sense are in short supply in some circles!

5. What is our evaluation of children and family? Is our approach: "We can't afford kids" – or, "We are going to wait a few years, enjoy lots of travel and fun without the burden

and expense of children? Maybe we'll get round to having family and stuff later." Such a hedonistic view may not work out. Keep in mind, that despite modern medical technological advances, allowing some women to give birth at a later age, normally children are born to younger parents. If you don't understand why, then ask most grandparents about the evident wisdom of such an arrangement! God knew what he was doing when he set the reproductive process in motion.

Furthermore, the idea that children are to be factored into financial planning suggests a misdirected sense of values. Who says you can cope with family only if you have enough money in the bank? Or whoever suggested that only children raised in moneyed homes have a corner on success? Quite often such children are indulged and end up becoming the brats of society. They've had everything dished up on a silver platter, so think that's what life is all about.

6. Here is a related question, "Can we afford not to have children?" There are great blessings, joys and discoveries to be shared by all, as children arrive in the home. If funds, space and other things are at a premium, so what? Those of us reared in less affluent, but loving homes, certainly have happy memories of sharing and enjoying the simple pleasures and toys of life, even if they were home-made. Whatever advances our bought-pleasure oriented society has made during the last half century, they have not resulted in more satisfaction or contentment - quite the opposite. In any case, we do not call the shots. We are not the masters of our own destiny - God is! To put off having a family for selfish reasons may unfortunately result in our not being able to have family at all! We may discover all too late that we, who thought we had a handle on everything, including our procreative timetable and potential, are not as smart as we thought.

7. Are we ready to handle disappointment?

Suppose things do not work out the way we expected. What if, despite careful family planning and good medical prognoses, we are unable to have children? What then? Will we still be quite happy with each other? Are we prepared to accept this possibility? Will one partner blame the other or even decide to opt out, for greener pastures? These are certainly considerations to keep in mind.

What if, God forbid, our offspring arrives physically, mentally or emotionally impaired? It may be patently clear that the child we have brought into the world needs the kind of specialised care we are unable to provide. What will we do? It is not always possible to anticipate such heart-breaking situations; life sometimes deals heavy blows. When it does, will we blame God, each other, or our forebears? Or will we cast ourselves on God and seek his help and grace?

8. If a couple discovers through prenatal research that the child they are expecting is likely to be impaired, will they be seriously tempted to accept the 'final solution' of our abortion-on-demand, convenience-first culture and opt to terminate the pregnancy? Or will they trust God for his very special enabling and offer their love unreservedly, come what may?

These are just a few of the questions which, although more easily asked than answered, are to be faced up to. As I write, I am both saddened and heartened as I recall friends, both old and young, who have been called to wade the deep waters of family disappointment and tragedy. They will tell us there are no easy answers. However, despite their tears and broken hearts, we have seen believers not only survive these dreadful trials, but mature into compassionate comforters of other sufferers. We can only stand back and wonder at God's amazing grace and the courage of his children.

Let us ever remember that God is still in the business of blessing families. He is personally concerned about yours.

His Word is still a safe guide; a great source of strength and consolation. As Job assures us - "...he knows the way that I take; when he has tried me, I shall come out as gold." - Job 23:10.

CHAPTER EIGHT

Look Out World, Here I Come!
(The First Baby)

What could be more exciting than welcoming the first baby? Most parents agree, "Babies are wonderful - particularly if they sleep at night!" Of course, let's face it, sleepless nights are par for the course in the early days following baby's arrival. During that initial period it's good to keep those words of scripture in mind - remember? "It came to pass," and, "nevertheless afterwards."

Despite the disturbances, be assured, child-rearing pays tremendous dividends - if not immediate financial ones! It is often said, "Babies bring their love with them." How true! What would life be like without the joys of little ones and family experiences? What a privilege to be able to shape and guide a small person who may one day be used to change the course of history. You never know what may be the result of your nurturing that baby boy or girl. Be sure to read the words spoken by the angel, Gabriel, to the old priest, Zacharias, prior to the birth of his son, John the Baptiser – Luke 1:11-17.

Preparing for the Big Day

As in many other areas of life, preparing for Junior's arrival is half the fun and very important. Parents need to prepare themselves. This includes our personal attitudes. It means, among other things, realising that life will never be the same again. Up to this point the couple have only had themselves to consider when making decisions. They have enjoyed freedom to travel, to go out for romantic evenings, to visit with friends and to spend their money on those little extras. Once 'his or her majesty' arrives on the scene, things will be different. However, remember, there will be great, life-enriching experiences you cannot afford to miss.

'Things'

This is the place to say something more about 'money and things'. We have looked at this elsewhere, but a reminder will not come amiss. Two extremes are best avoided; they are worry and indulgence. On the one hand, we must guard against undue worry about finances. As long as we are responsible and try to make ends meet, we can relax and live each day confidently. If we are able to set a little aside for our children's future educational needs, so well and good. By the way, there are agencies that can help in this regard. However, keep in mind the saying, "easy come, easy go." Wise parents teach their children about the value of work and money management and so help them to be better equipped for life and its challenges.

While we desire the best for our kids, the attitude: "Only the *very best* will do for *our* children" is not always helpful. Some parents knock themselves out trying to provide every last extravagance for their children. Remember, affluence can be as much a hindrance as a blessing in the development of our children's lives. Like their parents, children do not need all of the latest electronic gadgetry and games to get by in life. As Christian parents, let's remember, all we have and are, we hold in trust as God's stewards. Second, keep in mind that one of the great names of God is *Jehovah Jireh*, which means, 'the Lord will provide' or, as in another translation, 'the Lord will see to it'. God loves you and your family. Count on it! As in so many areas of life, balanced thinking is the key. Keep in mind that little saying, "God feeds the sparrows but He does not put it in their beaks."

Willing to Learn?

Before their first baby comes many young couples tend to think they have all the answers. They look at other people's families and wonder to each other: "How can people possibly be so disorganised?"

"How come Tom and Mary are so inept at handling crises? They panic even when their baby sneezes!"

"Why in the world don't Joe and Anne discipline their children more firmly?"

"Why are those people such stay-at-homes?"

It is surprising how our perspectives change after 'B-Day'! If you wonder what changed, it helps to take another look in the mirror.

You're Normal!

Speaking of attitudes, please understand that it is O.K. for new parents to be tired. It's not unspiritual to be a little impatient or even a bit irritable at times. There is a limit to physical stamina. Emotional stress thresholds vary, too. Surprise! You are not 'Superman' and 'Bionic Woman'. You are two ordinary people replete with all those regular human foibles and limits. Believe me, there will be days when you feel like opening the door and yelling out to no-one in particular: "Stop the world, I want to get off!" This, too, will pass. Of course, be sure to recognise any real physical or emotional problems and immediately seek professional help. Remember, Jesus said that sick people need a doctor - cf. Matthew 9:12. I'll take His advice anytime over that of some misguided, heal-on-demand televangelist!

Be sure to talk things through before baby arrives. Recognise that there will be sacrifices to be made. Accept the fact three can't live as cheaply as two - nor are they 'cheaper by the dozen'! Face it; if life and home become a bit more muddled and unpredictable, it's not the end of the world. Baby is far more important than things and tidy rooms. Knowing that everything is 'shipshape and Bristol fashion' may be vital for seamen but not necessarily for new parents! Any baby will tell you, cuddles are more important than muddles. Of course, having said that, it's a good idea to be reasonably organised; to know where Baby's bottle is - especially when he's trying to tell you he's hungry, at midnight! Furthermore, know where to find a clean diaper – or even where to dispose of the used one!

Taking Care of 'Mum-to-be'

Obviously this is priority number one. Fortunately, these days, all sorts of expert antenatal and postnatal care aids and practical advice are available, at least in our developed societies. It is wise to avail ourselves of whatever help is at hand, particularly that offered by the family doctor, the visiting nurse, the social worker and their associates.

By the same token, there is no need to be over-anxious. Most healthy women have nothing to fear. As my Dad reminded me when I was anxiously waiting for my beloved Audrey to deliver our older son, "Child-bearing is a perfectly natural process." Of course, there are due cautions to be observed. Alcohol, tobacco, drugs, certain foods and drinks are best avoided, as is undue stress. There are plenty of pamphlets and books that offer guidelines in these matters. Exercise, rest, relaxation and nourishment are important, but love and consideration are absolute necessities for MTBs (mums to be). A happy, cherished, relaxed woman who knows she is her husband's pride and joy will usually safely survive childbirth and bear well-adjusted children.

As Christians, let us keep in mind those most heartening words of the Apostle Paul who, writing to women in the early days of Christianity, said: "Yet she will be saved through childbearing-if they continue in faith and love and holiness, with self-control." – 1 Timothy 2:15.

Hebrew traditions surrounding childbirth are most interesting. Just six weeks after her delivery, the mother brought her child to the Lord in an act of thanksgiving and consecration – see Luke 2:22-24; cf. Leviticus 12.

Here are the words of the prayer at the conclusion of the service known as "The Churching of Women," found in the *Book of Common Prayer*:

"O Almighty God, we give thee humble thanks for thou hast vouchsafed to deliver this woman thy servant from the great pain and peril of child-bearing. Grant we beseech thee, most merciful Father, that she, through thy help, may both faithfully live and walk according to thy will, in this life present; and also may be partaker of everlasting glory in the life to come; through Jesus Christ our Lord. Amen."

What about Dad?

As far as Dad is concerned, he hasn't too much to fear! My father-in-law wrote to advise me, a long time ago, on the occasion mentioned above: "Cheer up, John; they haven't lost a father yet!" The important thing is for the dad-to-be to be thoughtful, considerate and kind – of course that goes for all husbands. It is of paramount importance that the dad is completely one with his wife in this special moment of their lives. Whether he is actually present at the birth is a matter for careful thought and choice, especially if Dad tends to pass out at the sight of blood! Delivery room personnel generally have enough on their plate without having to look after unscheduled patients.

That reminds me of an amusing incident our son was involved in. He was one of the attending physicians as the delivery room team prepared to perform two caesarean sections. When everything was in place, one of the nurses went to fetch one of the fathers who wished to be present at the birth of his child. Duly masked and gowned, the man was instructed to hold his wife's hand and try to say some encouraging words. All went well and the baby was safely delivered. The only problem was that the nurse, in her haste, had brought in the wrong dad! Unaware of the *faux pas*, the mum, still a little sleepy, thought it was so kind of the hospital to provide an extra doctor just to hold her hand. Mum's the word!

Pray Together

It goes without saying that Christian couples will recognise the need to prepare themselves spiritually for the advent of family. Those nine months of waiting for the big event afford opportunities to think, read and pray. Such times may not be as readily available once baby comes.

Reading the Scriptures together and finding out what helped Bible families to succeed or fail will be useful. Taking time to read good Christian books about child-nurturing and family life will also prove valuable. Most church libraries carry helpful material in these areas.

Praying together will be a truly bonding experience - especially praying out loud together. It may be a bit embarrassing at first but it will grow on you and be good training for the time when you pray together as a family. Incidentally, be sure to make that time for daily 'family prayers'.

Christian Counsel Helps

Be sure to seek the counsel and help of experienced Christian friends. It's surprising how many of the problems we face, as well as the questions we ask, have been met by others who have travelled along life's journey before us. There is no virtue in trying to go it alone or in 're-inventing the wheel', so to speak. Hopefully your church will offer teaching and make practical provision for young parents and families. If you can enlist the prayer support of some of the seniors and widows in your congregation, you will be truly blessed.

Church Involvement

Much could be said regarding the church's involvement with new parents and their children but space forbids. Whatever their tradition, most churches have services of thanksgiving and dedication for new babies. Some involve the extended family; some include people who are designated as 'godparents'. Some years ago I was present at a service where a couple who had newly come to faith in Christ stood before the congregation - at their own request - with all their children and were prayed for. It was especially moving to see individual members of the church stand beside each child and pledge to be a 'prayer parent' for that child. What a wonderful commitment and how strengthening for both church and family!

Practical Items

This book is not a handbook about child-raising; however, a few practical pointers may help. While caring for Baby may tend to become a full-time preoccupation, new parents must still try to find time for each other. Both need their rest, their quiet moments and their special times together. Baby will be very demanding but it will quickly become obvious that there is a difference between needs and wants. You will quickly learn to tell the difference, from the tone and decibels of baby's crying and occasional screams! You will find that while some noises call for thoughtful response, others are often best ignored.

Since, in the early days, Baby will spend quite a lot of time sleeping (sometimes, surprisingly, at the same time as the other family members), it will be helpful for him or her to have a separate space. If your circumstances are limited, don't feel that you must provide a fancy decorated nursery, complete with an expensive crib and extras. Lots of happy, healthy babies have slept in a drawer – open, of course! - or even in padded laundry baskets – I know from experience! You will quickly learn that not every cough, bump or sneeze is an emergency. It's surprising how noisy a baby can be even when sleeping. Generally speaking, as long as they are well-fed, dry and breathing fresh air, babies do just fine. As already noted, Mum and Dad need their rest too.

Well, lots more could be said but space is limited. Concerned parents will soon discover what their priorities are, especially as they learn to cast themselves on the Lord for his direction and help. Quite apart from its serious side, raising a baby can be fun - ask any grandma!

CHAPTER NINE

The Family, in Old Testament Times

Although they lived and wrote a long time ago, we can learn a lot about family life from the Old Testament writers. They saw the family not only as the basic building block of society, but as the training ground for life and responsibility within the community. Jewish families were, of course, very aware of their roots and heritage. This is particularly obvious from the several genealogical tables found in the Old Testament. We see also that parents often named their children after illustrious members of their own tribe. For example, Saul of Tarsus was no doubt named for his famous Benjamite ancestor, King Saul. The Hebrews clearly set great store by the family.

Children, a Gift from God

In Bible times children were said to be God's gift to the family and they were to be protected and nurtured in the faith. Remember these famous words from the Psalmist, cited earlier?

"Behold, children are a heritage from the Lord, the fruit of the womb a reward. Like arrows in the hand of a warrior are the children of one's youth. Blessed is the man who fills his quiver with them!" - Psalm 127:3-5.

Two other Scriptures come to mind. Here is Eve's response to the birth of Cain: "I have produced a man with the help of the Lord." - Genesis 4:1. Then there is God's promise to Abraham regarding Sarah: "I will bless her, and moreover, I will give you a son by her. I will bless her, and she shall become nations; kings of peoples shall come from her." - Genesis 17:16; cf. Genesis 29:32-34 and Ruth 4:11,12.

This idea of children being a special mark of divine favour is confirmed further by what the Bible says about barrenness and sterility. Strange though this may sound to us, not to have children was regarded as a mark of disgrace, if not divine displeasure. Listen to these sad words of Rachel, "She said to Jacob, 'Give me children, or I shall die!' Jacob's anger was kindled against Rachel, and he said, 'Am I in the place of God, who has withheld from you the fruit of the womb?' " - Genesis 30:1; cf. also v. 22-23; 1 Samuel 1:5,11; Isaiah 54:1.

We see that childbirth was a very special event and a time of community rejoicing in Israel. It involved, as well, some special ritual requirements for parents. (See Leviticus 12:3-8; Ruth 4:13-17.) The dedication and presentation of offspring, and the redemption of the firstborn were also ways of expressing gratitude to God and a sense of the family's dependence on him.

Here again are the well-known words from the story of the Baby Jesus' dedication: "And at the end of eight days, when he was circumcised, he was called Jesus...And when the time came for their purification according to the Law of Moses, they brought him up to Jerusalem to present him to the Lord (as it is written in the Law of the Lord, 'Every male who first opens the womb shall be called holy to the Lord') and to offer a sacrifice according to what is said in the Law of the Lord, 'a pair of turtle-doves, or two young pigeons.' " - Luke 2:21-24.

Instruction of Children
The Old Testament lays great stress on the parents' duty to instruct their children in spiritual matters. For example, when the great *Shema*, that most fundamental statement of Jewish belief, was pronounced, it was accompanied by the command:

"Hear, O Israel: The Lord our God, the Lord is one. You shall love the Lord your God with all your heart and with all your soul and with all your might. And these words that I command you today shall be on your heart. You shall teach them diligently to your children, and shall talk of them when you sit in your house, and when you walk by the way, and when you lie down, and when you rise." - Deuteronomy 6:4-7.

These words suggest several things. First, parents must make sure their children understand the nature of God. Second, children must be well instructed in the great principles of the Torah (the law of God given to Moses). Third, this training must be given along with consistent parental example. Jewish parents believed that the study of their nation's history not only made their children aware of God's providence but gave them a sense of participation in God's acts. This, of course, was particularly true in regard to the great Passover celebration, still treasured by Jewish families today. As each family sits at the Passover table listening to the recitation of the Haggadic narrative and sharing the roast lamb and other items, they are not just remembering but having a part in a live, historic ritual – cf. Exodus 12:25-27; Psalm 78:2-4 and Proverbs 22:6. Children are not only to be present at the Passover table but expected to take audible part in the ceremony, by asking leading questions of their father.

As we reflect on this careful and consistent instruction, we can begin to understand why the writer of Proverbs can promise: "Train up a child in the way he should go; even when he is old he will not depart from it." - Proverbs 22:6.

Respect and Concern for Parents

The Old Testament is not only clear in its instruction to parents, but also in its advice to children, instructing them to respect their parents. Indeed, at the very heart of the Ten Commandments we find these words: "Honour your father and your mother, that your days may be long in the land that the Lord your God is giving you." - Exodus 20:12. In the society of that day parents were regarded as visible stand-ins for God. Filial respect was seen as being akin to worship and not to be divorced from it. Both Jesus and the Apostle Paul cite the fifth commandment in support of their own teaching on the family – see Matthew 15:4 and Ephesians 6:1-3 - cf. Proverbs 1:7-9; 6:20-22; 23:22.

This mutual respect for parents and children accounts to a large degree for the stability and strength of Bible families. Granted, some of them were hardly exemplary, but on the whole those families can certainly teach us 'sophisticated moderns' a thing or two. In fact, even today, traditional Jewish families do not appear to experience the alienations and breakups so common in western society, at least, not to the same degree.

Correction and Punishment of Children

Again, we find that the Old Testament writers stress the need not only to instruct children but to require them to obey. Where such teaching is refused, or where there is disobedience, then there must be discipline and correction. This correction may take the form of corporal punishment. And, far from the authorities meddling or seeking to usurp parental authority in these matters, as is so common today, in those more enlightened times parental correction was supported by community leaders.

We may well give careful heed to these passages from Proverbs: "Whoever spares the rod hates his son, but he who loves him is diligent to discipline him." - Proverbs 13:24. "Folly is bound up in the heart of a child, but the rod of discipline drives it far from him." - Proverbs 22:15. "Do not withhold discipline from a child; if you strike him with a rod, he will not die." - Proverbs 23:13, cf. 29:15, 17.

Whatever we may think of this scriptural teaching and however we may respond to it in our own family situation is of course a matter of choice. However, there is no denying that the results of the neglect of these guidelines are painfully evident in our own confused, undisciplined, 'politically correct' society, with its total disrespect for authority of any kind. Surely we could do far worse than turn back the clock for once and listen to the wisdom of the ages. Of course, it goes without saying, that the Bible never condones the harsh or cruel treatment of children, quite the reverse.

CHAPTER TEN

Jesus and His Earthly Family

As we consider our Lord's teaching about family life we will look at two areas of his ministry. First, there is the informative narrative concerning Jesus' relationship with his own earthly family. Second, there are his practical, dependable guidelines for family life in general. In this chapter we will be concerned with his life.

Jesus and His Family

The central event of Scripture is the miracle of the Incarnation. Here, in time and space, is "God...manifest in the flesh." - 1 Timothy 3:16 KJV. Aside from the theological significance of the Incarnation, this is the story of how God came to live in the context of an ordinary earthly family. We call it the Nativity Story, but it is much more than that. It begins with the birth of Jesus but goes on to show us how he, who was truly God yet truly man, lived for thirty years in the setting of a modest, loving, earthly home. Consider some of the valuable lessons this most wonderful 'human story' can teach us.

The Value of Family Heritage

Jesus' family tree, presented with different emphases by Matthew and Luke, are not just literary 'fillers', nor fictitious attempts to humanise a supernatural person. They offer an accurate history of Jesus' human forebears. These written records remind us that Christianity is grounded in history, not mythology – see Matthew 1:1-17 and Luke 3:23-37. True, Jesus was miraculously conceived by the Holy Spirit and born of the Virgin Mary, but he was nonetheless a real 'flesh and blood baby', and a member of an earthly family.

We learn further, from Matthew's genealogical table, that while Jesus was part of a real human family tree, he was not limited by his heredity. From a Jewish point of view, it was unusual that four other women, apart from Mary, were mentioned in Jesus' genealogical record, especially since each of the four was of questionable repute for one reason or another. This fact should encourage us to understand that we are not inescapably determined by our heredity whether for good or ill. We can be grateful for our family heritage, but we must also remember that whatever else we inherit with our genes, we do not inherit God's salvation. That blessing depends on whether we personally accept the grace of God offered through the person and saving work of Christ.

Jesus and the Extended Family
Our Lord's earthly family heritage reminds us again of the great value of the extended family. It must have been a very difficult time for Mary as she awaited the birth of the baby Jesus. What she knew about her baby's supernatural conception would have sounded very strange to her family and friends. Living as she did in a close-knit village community, it would have been impossible for Mary to escape the questions and gossip of her neighbours.

Was it this situation that influenced Mary's mother - known traditionally as 'Anne' - to take her daughter to her cousin Elizabeth's home at *Ein Kerem*, a village in the Judean hills, near Jerusalem? Elizabeth herself was six months pregnant, despite her advanced years. This miracle in itself must have encouraged Anne to accept Mary's unusual explanation of her own condition. We can only conjecture – see Luke 1:39-45.

In any case, Mary's going to Elizabeth and Zacharias's home served several purposes. First, it meant that the aged Elizabeth had the benefit of the younger Mary's help in the final three months, as she awaited the birth of her son, John the Baptist. Elizabeth's husband, Zacharias, was too old to be of much practical assistance, especially in light of his temporary inability to speak. Under these circumstances, Mary's presence would have been most helpful. On the other hand, Zacharias's home provided a haven for Mary. Furthermore, Elizabeth would have sustained Mary and cheered her up during her pregnancy. There's nothing quite like the extended family when you need help.

Then there was the miracle that happened as Mary arrived on Elizabeth's doorstep. That, together with Elizabeth's inspired greeting, must have been further confirmation for Mary of Gabriel's earlier annunciation. It would certainly have shown both Elizabeth and Anne that Mary was the object of God's special favour. This beautiful little story illustrates once again the kind of mutual consideration and comfort available within an extended family.

We note one other telling incident in the story of Jesus' extended family. It happened while Jesus was hanging on the Cross. Despite his own suffering, he was concerned for his mother Mary. We hear him very tenderly commit her into the care of his disciple, John. It is generally accepted that John, like his brother James, was the son of Mary's sister, Salome - cf. John 19:25; Mark 15:40; Mathew 27:56. If we are right in our understanding of this relationship, then at the end of his earthly life, as at its beginning, Jesus recognised the helpfulness of the wider family circle.

The Significance and Worth of Human Antenatal Life
The story of Mary's visit to Elizabeth's home can also help us in the current controversy about abortion and attitudes toward unborn children. This is how Luke, himself a physician, describes what happened,

"And when Elizabeth heard the greeting of Mary, the baby leaped in her womb. And Elizabeth was filled with the Holy Spirit, and she exclaimed with a loud cry, 'Blessed are you among women, and blessed is the fruit of your womb! And why is this granted to me that the mother of my Lord should come to me? For behold, when the sound of your greeting came to my ears, the baby in my womb leaped for joy. And blessed is she who believed that there would be a fulfilment of what was spoken to her from the Lord.' " - Luke 1:41-45.

Whether we wish to explain this event in physiological, psychological, or spiritual terms, one thing is evident. Luke, a doctor, described what was in Elizabeth's womb as a 'baby', not merely a 'foetus'. For him, here was a human being, capable of sensation and intelligent response. No doubt Elizabeth was given special supernatural insight. The significant movement of the child in her womb confirmed this revelation to her. Furthermore, Elizabeth's greeting of Mary as "mother of my Lord" tells us that although Mary was in the very initial stage of her own pregnancy, she too was carrying a real human child. One wonders what might have happened if either Mary or Elizabeth had opted for an abortion. Either of them might have argued, at least in the idiom of today's abortion-on-demand proponents, that they had 'grounds for therapeutic abortions'. Their social and religious training, not to mention their personal faith in God, helped them to think in much more wholesome terms. They were filled with thanksgiving and praise to God for his goodness. Any doubt we may have about this is quickly dispelled if we read Mary's beautiful *Magnificat* (Luke 1:46-55).

Many well-meaning people, unfortunately some Christians among them, still entertain the unscriptural notion that marriage and procreation are God's second best. As we noted earlier, even the Christian church, in its history, has tended to glorify celibacy and question the propriety of marriage and healthy sexual relationships. Even such notables as the lawyer, Tertullian, and the theologian, Augustine of Hippo, spoke of marriage as if it were 'legalised adultery'. Incidentally, even today, we are seeing the tragic consequences, not to mention the shame being brought on Christianity in general, by the promiscuous behaviour of hundreds of Roman Catholic priests, who are frustrated by their church's unnatural and unscriptural demand for celibacy. The story of the birth and life of Jesus certainly repudiates such false notions.

Granted, Jesus was born of a virgin and not as a result of the normal, procreative process. Nevertheless, he was physically born from the womb of Mary. Then she, in accordance with Jewish custom and procedure, went through the usual purification ceremony associated with childbirth. What is more, according to the Bible, after Jesus' birth, Mary and her husband Joseph became the parents of several children. (Matthew 1:25; Mark 6:3; John 7:5) In other words, the Nativity story encourages us to recognise that marriage, procreation, and responsible family life are perfectly normal and a part of God's plan for humanity.

The Importance of Parental Piety
We know very little about the private lives of Mary and Joseph. However, from what we are told about them in Scripture, we know that they were exemplary in their piety. They evidently ordered their lives in accordance with the directions and requirements of the Word of God - especially in the matter of Jesus' childhood – cf. Luke 2:22-24, 27, 39, 42. It was certainly no accident that Jesus was born and raised in the family and home of people like Joseph and Mary. Although nothing like the supernatural beings so fancifully portrayed by some elements of Christendom, here were two special people of faith.

Mary was obviously a very spiritually mature girl. In keeping with the custom of that day, she had been promised and betrothed to Joseph. This contract might well have been made when Mary was quite young, then, in accordance with custom, confirmed when she was of responsible age. The emphasis placed on the betrothal of Joseph and Mary in the Nativity story indicates that they both agreed to the betrothal with its ensuing responsibilities and ultimate consummation in marriage.

They would have understood that their betrothal could only be dissolved by a proper divorce (Matthew 1:19).

Luke speaks of Mary's purity. She was still a virgin (*parthenos*) when she received the angel Gabriel's announcement. This does not mean simply that she was a 'young woman of marriageable age', as liberal commentators argue. Had Luke meant that - Greek scholar that he was - he would have used the word *neants*. Of course, Gabriel's words to Mary tell us that she was the recipient of God's grace. By the way, it is unfortunate that the Greek word *kecharitomene* is mistranslated by the well-known Latin phrase *gratia plena*, which in turn, becomes in English, 'full of grace'. Gabriel did not in fact say that Mary was a *source* of grace but a *recipient* of it. As one famous commentator put it, "Mary was not the mother of grace but a daughter of grace!" Whatever else these words tell us, they give us to understand that Mary's heart was open to receive the Lord's blessing. Not only was she a girl of great faith who took God at his word, but one who was totally available to be the instrument of the Holy Spirit (Luke 1:35, 45; Matthew 1:20). However, despite her unique experience and exemplary life, the Bible nowhere suggests that she was sinless, nor does it offer the slightest support for the mischievous doctrine of her 'immaculate conception'. Strikingly, Mary herself tells us that she rejoiced in "*God my Saviour!*" (Luke 1:47).

Joseph receives rather brief notice in the Nativity story. He himself must have been a man of unusual faith who accepted God's word under the most difficult of circumstances (Matthew 1:20-25). Imagine how he must have felt upon discovering that Mary was pregnant. Despite this heart-rending situation, Joseph's kindly spirit overcame any feeling of hatred or vindictiveness. Still unaware of the facts, as later explained to him by the Angel of the Lord, Joseph decided that instead of subjecting Mary to public disgrace, he would quietly divorce her, in accordance with Jewish law regarding a broken engagement. Once made aware of Mary's miracle, Joseph obeyed the Angel, married Mary, and thus became, by that act, the legal father of her expected child.

It seems he had the privilege of naming the baby 'Jesus' (v.25). Significantly, the angel addressed him as, "Joseph, son of David." In Matthew's official genealogy Jesus' ancestry is traced back through Joseph to David.

The faith and kindness of Joseph are everywhere evident in the Nativity story, as in the unfolding story of our Lord's life. For example, although he married Mary and took her to his home, prior to the actual birth of Jesus, Joseph carefully and patiently refrained from physical union with her until after her baby was born. Then when later the baby Jesus' life was threatened by the cruel scheme of Herod the Great (Matthew 2:16), it was Joseph who, in obedience to another divine revelation, courageously took Mary and her baby by night to a safe refuge in Egypt.

Upon the death of Herod, Joseph discreetly returned with Mary and Jesus to a remote area of Nazareth in Galilee. There, in that unlikely place, Joseph followed his trade as a carpenter and provided for his family. As Jesus grew into boyhood and young manhood it would appear that he served his apprenticeship under Joseph. This is implied in the question asked in Mark 6:3, "Is not this the carpenter, the son of Mary...?" It seems Joseph died while Jesus was young, but not before he had spent long hours with his 'son' at the carpenter's bench. As a responsible parent, Joseph had trained Jesus in the skills of his craft.

Joseph and Mary as Parents

Having considered their individual commitments to God, we now look at Mary and Joseph as husband and wife together and see how they accepted the responsibility of parenthood. The first thing we notice is their submission to Scripture. For example, on the eighth day of Jesus' life Joseph and Mary took him to Jerusalem to have him circumcised in accordance with the law of Moses (Leviticus 12:3). Then about a month later, thirty-three days, according to the law (Leviticus 12:4), they were at the Temple again, this time "to present him to the Lord" and thus comply with the law's requirements for the consecration of the firstborn (Luke 2:22-24; cf. Exodus 13:2-12). Their offering on this occasion indicates that they were poor people (Leviticus 12:8). It must have been a wonderful occasion for both of them as they listened to the prophetic utterances spoken about Jesus by the aged Simeon and Anna.

Another indication of their being good parents is their appreciation of what we might call today 'family church life'. Luke tells us, for example, how Joseph and Mary joined in the annual Passover pilgrimage to Jerusalem. Since they lived in Nazareth, traveling to Jerusalem would have involved a three day journey on foot. While we are not told specifically that they took Jesus with them on these occasions, almost certainly they did. We do know that when he was twelve years old he went with them to Jerusalem, no doubt, this time, for his 'bar mitzvah'. This was the visit when Jesus remained in the temple to discuss the Law with the teachers. Evidently Joseph and Mary's parental vigilance lapsed on this occasion and it took them three days to find Jesus. When they did find him they learned further lessons about his divine origin and mission (Luke 2:41-51).

The story of Jesus' special visit to the synagogue in Nazareth, following his baptism and temptation, throws some light on his home life. We read, "And he came to Nazareth, where he had been brought up. And *as was his custom*, he went to the synagogue on the Sabbath day, and he stood up to read." (Luke 4:16). Evidently Joseph and Mary had not only taken care of Jesus physically, but spiritually as well. They had, despite their poverty, made sure that their son was versed in the scriptures. Of course, not only did Jesus learn from Mary and Joseph, but they were able to learn much from him. It is important for parents not only to teach and direct their children in the ways of the Lord but to be willing to learn from them as well. Such are the blessings of a godly home.

We can learn many lessons about family from Jesus' life in Nazareth. There are few more beautiful word cameos than the one painted in Luke 2:51; "And he went down with them and came to Nazareth and was submissive to them. And his mother treasured up all these things in her heart. And Jesus increased in wisdom and in stature and in favour with God and man." In this snapshot from the teenage years of Jesus we see an example for all young people. We note also that Jesus was perfectly content to spend his early years in Nazareth, of all places. He submitted to his parents' wishes. As he grew in body so he grew in mind and spirit.

Jesus also took his full share of responsibility around the home. Here was one teenager who learned the disciplines of hard work. As noted above, it is possible that Joseph died quite young. At least he disappears completely from the pages of Scripture. This would mean that Jesus became his mother's supporter and the breadwinner in the family while he was still quite young. What we read about some members of Jesus' earthly family suggests they were not the most congenial or cooperative group (John 7:5; Matthew 13:57; Mark 3:21). Jesus' care for his mother during his life, and even at the time of his death (John 19:27), offers a lovely example of the concern children should have for their aged parents.

The Blessing of Marriage and Home

A beautiful passage in the Book of Common Prayer reads,
'Holy matrimony...which holy estate Christ adorned and beautified with His presence, and first miracle that He wrought in Cana of Galilee.'
(The Form of Solemnization of Matrimony)

We learn further lessons about family life from this story of Jesus' first miracle (John 2). For example, we see that our Lord recognised the importance of the marriage celebration. Today, in some circles, we hear people stating their preference for 'common law' living, or 'living together'. For them the idea of a formal marriage is *passé*. It is good to remember that Jesus stamps his approval and blessing on marriage, not only by his presence but by performing his first miracle at the one in Cana. A wedding service demonstrates our belief in commitment, covenant, faithfulness, and legality.

Jesus' miracle at this wedding assures us that, among other things, he approves of our being happy. Not only is he willing to meet human emergencies but to show his power on behalf of ordinary people. It is so easy to think of Jesus in terms of religion and church. It is much more important to see that he is with us in our homes and concerned about the everyday problems that we face in our family circle.

Our Lord's appreciation of home life and the understanding of human relationships is also seen in other of his miracles. For example, he restored Peter's wife's mother (Matthew 8:14). He gave a daughter back to her bereaved parents (Luke 8:40-56). He cast out a demon and healed the daughter of the Syrophoenician woman (Mark 7:26-30). He healed a demoniac boy and an official's son, restoring them to their respective fathers (Mark 9:17-27; John 4:46-54). He raised a widow's son and gave him back to her (Luke 7:11-17); and finally, he restored Lazarus to his home and sisters in Bethany (John 11:11-44).

Although he had no home of his own in adult life (Luke 9:58), Jesus was happy to enjoy the warmth and hospitality of other people's homes. We see him enjoying a visit to Peter's home at Capernaum (Matthew 8:14); dining in the home of his disciple, Matthew (Matthew 9:9, 10); accepting the hospitality of Simon the Pharisee (Luke 7:36); and welcomed as a guest in Zacchaeus' home at Jericho (Luke 19:1-7). The home of Mary, Martha and Lazarus in Bethany was one of his very favourite places (John 11:1-5). After his resurrection, one of his early 'appearances' took place in the home of the two disciples, at Emmaus (Luke 24:28-31).

While Jesus approved of and appreciated married life, he also recognised and demonstrated the possibility of fulfilment and happiness in the single life. Our Lord was not celibate to prove that such a life was more virtuous. His single state was part of the sacrifice he accepted as part of his unique commitment to the will of God, in the work of our salvation. He would allow nothing, not even usual human relationships, to distract him from his task.

We see then that Jesus' life on earth offers many helpful pointers for our own homes and family relationships. Let us never forget that he left the glory of his Father's eternal home and came to share fully in the life of an ordinary earthly family. He did this that we might be part of God's 'forever family' and share his heavenly home. This is all so beautifully expressed in the children's hymn:

> *I love to think though I am young,*
> *My Saviour was a child;*
> *That Jesus walked this earth along,*
> *With feet all undefiled.*
>
> *He kept His Father's word of truth*
> *As I am taught to do*
> *And while He walked the paths of youth,*
> *He walked in wisdom too.*
>
> *That He who wore the thorny crown*
> *And tasted death's despair,*
> *Had a kind mother like my own,*
> *And knew her love and care.*
>
> (E. Paxton Hood)

CHAPTER ELEVEN

Jesus Teaches about Family Matters

Jesus lived in a society that set great store by family life. In this area of life relationships, as in so many other social and ethical concerns, the Jews stood apart in the ancient world. Not only did they believe in the value of human life at all its stages, but emphasised the need for parental responsibility. What is more, they stressed the need for children to respect and take care of their aged parents. Although Jesus did not say a lot specifically on the subject of family, what he did say and imply is clear and will best be heeded.

The Value of Children

When Jesus was questioned by his disciples about greatness in the Kingdom of heaven, he called a little child and had him stand among them. He said:

"Truly, I say to you, unless you turn and become like children, you will never enter the kingdom of heaven. Whoever humbles himself like this child is the greatest in the kingdom of heaven. Whoever receives one such child in my name receives me, but whoever causes one of these little ones who believe in me to sin, it would be better for him to have a great millstone fastened round his neck and to be drowned in the depth of the sea." - Matthew 18:2-6.

It is surprising that these strong words of Jesus, among the harshest he uttered, should be spoken about the ill-treatment of children. Obviously he set great store by them and placed an eternal worth on them. He saw children as simple, uncomplicated, and trusting. A little later we hear him saying, "See that you do not despise one of these little ones. For I tell you that in heaven their angels always see the face of my Father who is in heaven." - Matthew 18:10.

Then there are his other famous words, "Let the little children come to me and do not hinder them, for to such belongs the kingdom of heaven." - Matthew 19:14.

These sayings of Jesus tell us just how much he appreciated little ones and how seriously he viewed adult and parental attitudes toward them. Grown-ups need to recognise how vulnerable children are. Parents will be wise to heed Jesus' stern warning about the dire consequences of hindering or causing a child to sin.

Bringing our children to Jesus
> "When Mothers of Salem
> Their children brought to Jesus,
> The stern disciples drove them back
> And bade them depart:
> But Jesus saw them 'ere they fled
> And sweetly smiled, and kindly said,
> Suffer little children to come unto Me."

These words from W.M. Hutching's children's hymn, based on Matthew 19:13-14, remind us of the importance of bringing our children to the Lord. Perhaps those 'Mothers of Salem' recognised Jesus for who he really was and sensed the great opportunity of letting their children meet him. How encouraged they must have been when Jesus, despite his disciples' gruffness, welcomed the little ones and placed his hands upon them in a gesture of blessing.

The Saviour's welcoming of the children is surely an encouragement for all Christian parents to bring their children to Jesus. This may be done in a number of ways. We bring them to him in the arms of our faith and prayer, asking his divine blessing and mercy to be upon them. We may also wish to do it more formally and publicly in a short service of dedication. In this way we not only express our thanks to God publicly but solicit the prayers of the members of our church on behalf of our family. This is certainly in line with Bible passages like 1 Samuel 1:28; Luke 2:27, 28; and Matthew 19:13-15.

Another way in which we bring our children to the Lord is by making sure there is a happy spirit of Christian love and nurture in our homes. Nothing can fully take the place of godly, parental example. This may include such things as a daily 'family altar' and instruction in the Word of God. But such influence goes beyond these things. We need to offer our children the security and support of our friendship.

It is not enough to drag them off to countless meetings at church. Of course, church should have an important place in the Christian family's schedule, but it is important to be home when needed and to exhibit and explain the love of Jesus in the everyday things of life. We must also be ready to give good answers to our children's sincere questions. We cannot guarantee that our children will be saved, nor be sure that they will grow up to live for the Lord. However, there is a sense in which we can trust our children into the safe hands of Christ, knowing that he cares as much for families as he does for individuals. The story of Susannah Wesley is a wonderful example for us. Despite having eighteen children, she took time regularly to pray and share the scriptures with each of them. The amazing story of John and Charles Wesley tell us how effective that godly woman's ministry was. Indeed, one historian said that the ministry of the Wesleys spared England from the French Revolution.

Providing Wisely

"Or which one of you, if his son asks him for bread, will give him a stone? Or if he asks for a fish, will give him a serpent? If you then, who are evil, know how to give good gifts to your children, how much more will your Father who is in heaven give good things to those who ask him!" - Matthew 7:9-11.

Although Jesus' main lesson here is about prayer and especially about God's grace in answering our payers, he is also pointing out parents' responsibility to make wise provision for their children. It is one thing to give gifts to our children; it is another thing to give them "good gifts". Jesus' words imply that it is a part of parenthood to know the difference.

Two extremes are best avoided. On the one hand, we must not short change our children; but on the other, we must not indulge them. In the above passage the two things asked for are simple items from the staple diet of the people of Galilee in the time of Jesus. In the home where Jesus grew up as a boy it is very doubtful whether there were many extras. People, whether adults or children, seem to have been content with the simple fare of life.

We get a similar picture in the story of the boy who gave his lunch to Jesus. His meal consisted of five small barley loaves and two small fish. Although Jesus multiplied the food so that it amply fed the entire multitude, we see that he made sure that there was no waste. Whatever was left over was collected and, no doubt, put to good use (John 6:8-13). I'm sure it wasn't dumped in the garbage, as so often happens in our wasteful society. How often do we spare a thought for the boy's mother who had wisely provided for her son's needs? We can be sure that Jesus not only thanked the lad but sent a word of thanks home to his mother, not to mention a special 'doggie bag' for her!

By contrast, we might recall the story of the prodigal son. While his spendthrift habits were inexcusable, his father's handing him the money to squander in the first place leaves plenty of room for questions. We might also catch a hint of parental favouritism from this story; at least that was how the elder son felt, rightly or wrongly. It is unfortunate that many parents today, in our pampered western society, think they have to satisfy their children's every whim and provide activities to fill every waking moment of their children's lives. Far better to let our children discover the fun of the simple, unbought pleasures of life for themselves.

In Jesus' parable about the 'friend at midnight', the man who provided the required bread can teach us some useful lessons about being provident. He had obviously made provision for his family and had bread enough and to spare. This father not only knew where his children were, but had made sure they were in bed, where children should be at midnight! He had also made sure that his house was secure against intruders. Those are good lessons for any parent to keep in mind.

Children's Care for Parents

It is clear, from Jesus' words spoken to the Jerusalem scribes and Pharisees, that he believed that caring for parents was more important than observing religious traditions. Listen to his words, "And why do you break the commandment of God for the sake of your tradition? For God commanded, 'Honour your father and your mother,' and, 'Whoever reviles father or mother must surely die.' But you say, 'If anyone tells his father or his mother, "What you would have gained from me is given to God," he need not honour his father.' So for the sake of your tradition you have made void the word of God." - Matthew 15:3-6.

Several things emerge from this passage. First, it is crystal clear that in quoting from the Ten Commandments Jesus accepted their universal validity as timeless, moral directives. For him, honouring and providing for parents in need was not just an option, it was a requirement of God's law. Any attempt to evade this law, even in the name of religion was wrong, as far as Jesus was concerned. What he was dealing with here was the Jewish custom of 'corban' - a quasi-religious banking system whereby funds could be deposited for safe-keeping in the Temple treasury. The money was thus made available for religious purposes but could be reclaimed on demand, in the event of an emergency - no doubt, with a small interest! Apparently there was a strange fiction that money on loan to God might secure some spiritual preferment, not to mention avoid assisting family members in their time of need. Jesus saw right through this subterfuge and taught the lesson that 'religious' excuses for not supporting needy parents are no better than any other kind. In fact he infers that there are few worse scams than religious ones. Unfortunately, there are still plenty around today!

In our welfare society, we need to remember Jesus' words. Children are unworthy who fail to care for and show love to their elderly parents. Whether we are parents or children, we need to keep in mind that practical, filial and family love are far more significant than any amount of religious profession, public service, or preaching. If we have any question about the things the Lord values, his teaching here indicates that he sets far more store by honesty than religious correctness.

Family and Spiritual Loyalties

Jesus warned against allowing earthly relationships to encroach on our commitment to God. He said, "If anyone comes to me and does not hate his own father and mother and wife and children and brothers and sisters, yes, and even his own life, he cannot be my disciple." - Luke 14:26. On the surface this certainly sounds like an impossible demand and might even be cited as warrant for the kind of selfish conduct we've just been considering. Fortunately, we have a parallel passage in Matthew's gospel which interprets Jesus' words for us: "Whoever loves father or mother more than me is not worthy of me, and whoever loves son or daughter more than me is not worthy of me." - Matthew 10:37. From this version of Jesus' words we discover that 'hate' in this context is a relative term. It does not mean 'hatred' as we usually think of it. Obviously that would be sin and would be condemned by Jesus himself, cf. Matthew 5:21, 22. What Jesus is saying in effect, is that our love for our family must not become idolatrous nor usurp the place of our love for God.

The time may come when relations may make demands of us that can only be met by our being disloyal to Christ. In this case, the line of duty is clear: the Lord must come first. If we find these demands of Jesus difficult, so be it. He is making it plain, that our commitment to him should not be frivolous or born of self-interest.

One of Jesus' parables talks about people who so lightly regarded the importance of the Kingdom of God and their eternal destiny that they used relatives as an excuse for not entering into it. For example, one man turned down the invitation to the great banquet on the basis that he had "married a wife." He made her the excuse for his own inexcusable rudeness, thus, in terms of the meaning of the parable, robbing both his wife and himself of the blessings of the Kingdom – cf. Luke 14:15ff.

When Jesus said to the would-be disciple who wanted first to go home and bury his father, "Let the dead bury their dead," he was not being callous. Jesus knew that if the man's father had in fact been lying dead at home, he would not have been allowed out of the house. The Lord saw through the man's excuse. What the fellow really meant was, he would go home, wait until his father died, pick up his share of the estate, then he might consider becoming a disciple of Jesus. That kind of self-love disqualifies a person from identifying with Jesus.

Jesus' teaching is carefully balanced. On the one hand, he urged care for family; but on the other, he warned against allowing family or even self-interest to trespass on the domain of our commitment to God. Of course, it goes without saying that a person who really understands the true meaning of Christian commitment is most likely to make a responsible parent or relative. Christianity surely must begin at home. So much then for Jesus' very down-to-earth, if demanding, teaching about family.

CHAPTER TWELVE

God's Gift of a Mother

There is no greater earthly treasure than a godly mother. Not only do we owe our very existence to our mothers, but they are the ones who dry our tears, calm our fears, teach us to walk and talk, pick us up when we fall down and love us even when we fail. They are also the ones who pray for us as long as God lends them breath. There is an apocryphal tale that, when God created the human race, he specially created mothers as his vice-regents, in order to help him take care of things.

Despite contemporary secularism's attempts to denigrate motherhood, most ordinary, sensible people recognise that there are few more wonderful privileges or responsibilities than that of being a mum. What sort of a home is it without a mother? As the saying goes, "Home is where mother is."

The Bible certainly sets great value on mothers. It portrays them as those who offer moral fibre and spiritual integrity to their children. Interestingly enough, a Jew's ethnicity is derived from his mother. Motherhood was, and still is in some societies, viewed as a singular mark of divine blessing, while barrenness was a sign of God's disfavour. Be that as it may, many women who have not been privileged to give birth to children have been renowned as 'mothers in Israel'. Only recently we received a touching photograph from a missionary who has established a family home for ten adopted African children, several of them orphaned by AIDS. Sitting with her husband, surrounded by her little charges, she had written the photo's caption, "Barren but bedecked with babies." Thank God for such people whose love for God has helped them turn disappointment into blessing and sadness into gladness!

Practical Problems

Before we look at the stories of some Bible mothers, let's look at a couple of problems facing many mothers today – some fathers too, for that matter!

What about working mothers?

This, of course, is a delicate question, not always easily answered. First of all, let's understand the question. Who in his right mind would ever suggest that a mother doesn't work? We are, of course, talking about mothers who for one reason or another work outside the home.

In ever-increasing numbers, mothers find themselves raising their families single-handedly and alone. They are thus obliged to find a job. This scenario is occasioned by a variety of situations, quite apart from things like divorce, desertion or drop-out dads. For example, a husband's illness, unemployment, or similar unexpected problems may preclude his being the gainfully-occupied breadwinner. We live in a time of social change, especially in industrialised societies.

Whereas Dad used to be the one who went out to work, while Mum stayed home to look after the children and other responsibilities, that is no longer the general pattern. As a result of technological advances, mega-mergers, or the need to compete in the global economy, many companies are streamlining or in a downsizing mode. As a result, all kinds of people are being laid off, even high profile, top flight executives. People who thought they were secure until retirement are told they no longer possess the required marketable skills and are being shown the door.

Quite apart from the social and psychological problems this creates, many a man is finding himself at home, caring for the family, cleaning and cooking, while his wife is out at work. This may or may not be ideal; it depends very much on a person's adaptability and attitude. Sometimes this switching of roles can be advantageous and bring about a special bonding between a father and his young children, as we have already observed.

Whatever the situation, the important thing, especially for younger children, is parental presence whenever possible. Day care facilities, pre-schools, nannies may be helpful, even necessary sometimes, but there is no substitute for Mum or Dad. There is a great sense of security for children who, when they burst through the door of their home with their expectant, "Hello, Mum," hear Mum's or Dad's response! Even if Mum has to go out to work, the trick is to try to be there when the children are there!

Often the key lies in our outlook and sense of values. As long as we keep the well-being of our children as our priority, other things usually fall into place. Christian mums will be well advised not to buy into the contemporary cultural myth that a mother's personal professional development and fulfilment are more important than her vocation to be a mother. That myth is not only contrary to biblical patterns, it creates tensions in a family. There is no higher calling than motherhood. Fortunately, and here is one benefit of modern technology, today many mothers are finding opportunities to work from their home office or are developing 'cottage industries'. This has the advantage of providing a living while being at home when family needs call for it.

What about the family's responsibility to Mum?

It goes without saying that, in the Christian family particularly, children are responsible to show their mother respect and to obey her. A mother will be wise to teach her family such things and to require such of them. Naturally, where there is a dad he will reinforce this by his example, as well as by precept. A husband who takes his wife for granted, or is uncaring and self-centred, frequently 'out with the boys', is unlikely to raise respectful children. Indeed, it has been wisely observed that the greatest gift a father can give his children is to love their mother. We may add: do not be afraid of showing your affection for each other in the presence of the children, it will bless them. Dads have special responsibilities. I remember a World War II, 'careless talk' warning we had in England, "Be like Dad, keep Mum!"

Of course, this question of responsibility involves adult children too. They have benefitted from their mother and father's care and support over the years - now it's time to reciprocate. To forget to show concern and love towards Mother, especially in her senior years is, to say the least, unpardonable. The Bible is unequivocal about this. This is what Paul has to say on the matter:

"But if a widow has children or grandchildren, let them first learn to show godliness to their own household and to make some return to their parents, for this is pleasing in the sight of God...if anyone does not provide for his relatives, and especially for members of his household, he has denied the faith and is worse than an unbeliever." - 1 Timothy 5:4-8.

These days there is no excuse for failing to communicate with parents. A telephone call, a little note, a Mother's Day card or an invitation for a meal can be a great cheer to a mum, particularly if she is now alone. It seems that sons need a special prod in this direction. Have you heard the little saying:
"A son is a son until he finds a wife;
A daughter is a daughter all her life?"

CHAPTER THIRTEEN

Six Famous Bible Mothers

Having considered the importance of motherhood and of appreciating and caring for our own mothers, we now look briefly at the stories of some famous Bible mothers and see what they have to teach us.

Eve

When Adam is introduced to his wife, in the Creation story, he names her *Ishah,* recognising that, although different from himself, she was, in a way, part of him. Here are Adam's words: "This at last is bone of my bones and flesh of my flesh; she shall be called Woman, because she was taken out of Man." - Genesis 2:23. As noted earlier, the Hebrew word translated 'man' is *Ish*, while the word for woman is *Ishah.* There is an obvious play on words here.

It was only subsequent to the disaster of the Fall that the woman received her personal name, 'Eve', the significance of which is explained by Adam himself. "The man called his wife's name Eve, because she was the mother of all living." - Genesis 3:20. Adam evidently understood that in the gracious purposes of God, despite his own and Eve's sin and its punishment, all was not lost. The human race would survive and his wife would be the mother of mankind; the archetype of motherhood.

Eve herself recognised that the ability to conceive was a gifting from the Lord and that life was ultimately in God's hand. She says: "I have produced (literally: 'acquired') a man with the help of the Lord." - Genesis 4:1. It is worth noting that while

Adam and Eve – together described as 'Adam' – were created "in the likeness of God", when Eve gives birth to Seth, her third son, he is said to be born "in [Adam's] own likeness, after his image"- Genesis 5:2-3. We are thus given to understand that, among other things, Adam and Eve jointly passed on a sinful heredity to their offspring.

We note in passing that Adam and Eve were both responsible regarding sin. This gives the lie to the teaching that Jesus' sinlessness was preserved by his birth of a virgin mother, without male involvement. The fact is that Mary, like every other human apart from Jesus himself, was a sinner who needed a Saviour; a fact she herself readily acknowledged– see Luke 1:47. Our Lord's sinlessness was guaranteed solely because of his being miraculously conceived of the Holy Spirit – see Matthew 1:20 and Luke 1:35. Furthermore, as we saw when we discussed the birth of Jesus, there is no biblical evidence for the doctrine of the 'immaculate conception' of Mary, the virgin mother of Jesus – a doctrine only promulgated in 1854.

Sarah

Here is another truly remarkable story of motherhood, described for us in the book of Genesis. Sarah, like Abraham her husband, was well beyond the age of child-bearing, yet in accordance with the divine promise she gave birth to Isaac, whose name means 'laughter'. Here is part of the story as told in the Bible:

"And Sarah conceived and bore Abraham a son in his old age...Sarah said, 'God has made laughter for me; everyone who hears will laugh over me.' And she said, 'Who would have said to Abraham that Sarah would nurse children? Yet I have borne him a son in his old age.' " - Genesis 21:2-7.

Although Sarah had at first laughed at the thought of giving birth to a child, she was a mother who displayed great faith, not only at the time of Isaac's conception but subsequently. There is an interesting verse in Hebrews chapter 11 that reads: "Through faith also Sarah herself received strength to conceive seed..." - v.11 (KJV).

Like most mothers, Sarah was very protective of her son, which was perfectly understandable in her particular situation. She made her feelings abundantly clear to her husband on the occasion of the feast that celebrated Isaac's weaning. When she saw Ishmael, Abraham's son by Hagar, Sarah's slave girl, making fun of the proceedings, she said to Abraham, "Cast out this slave woman with her son, for the son of this slave woman shall not be heir with my son Isaac." - Genesis 21:10.

Think too what it must have been like for Sarah when Abraham told her of God's call to offer Isaac as a burnt offering on Mount Moriah. How her mother's heart must have bled as she watched father and son set out on that fateful journey. How she must have rejoiced to see her boy return later. There's a hint in the beautiful love story of Isaac and Rebekah that Isaac and his mum had been very close. We read, "So Isaac was comforted after his mother's death." - Genesis 24:67.

Sarah's story is a great encouragement to all mothers, especially to any who are facing difficult, challenging times. Remember the Lord's own question to Abraham? "Is anything too hard for the Lord?" –Genesis 18:14.

Jochebed
Here is another mother whose faith was evident both in her courage and her ingenuity. Jochebed was the mother of Moses. Despite the cruel, genocidal edict of Pharaoh, this brave mother was determined to preserve her little son's life. After hiding the baby Moses for three months – no easy task, as any parent will tell you! – Jochebed constructed the waterproof papyrus basket and placed Moses in it, among the reeds beside the Nile.

She then sent Miriam, Moses' sister, to stand guard. Although we are not given the details, it's obvious that Jochebed displayed keen maternal common sense. First of all, if challenged by the authorities, she could say truthfully, "Yes, I have put my son in the river!" Second, she made sure she put him where he was most likely to be discovered – near the spot where the princess of Egypt came to bathe. Third, she made herself available as a nursemaid for the baby – not expecting to get paid a state family allowance!

We know little else about Jochebed's activities but we can rest assured she must have had a tremendous influence on Moses. Who do you suppose told him of his true identity and ethnicity? Who helped Moses cultivate a right sense of values? Who told him about Messiah? You can be sure it wasn't Pharaoh or his daughter!

Jochebed presents us with a shining example of a godly mother, praying over and preparing her son for God's service - cf. Exodus 2:1-10; Hebrews 11:23-27. No wonder Moses' parents are included in the roll-call of people of faith – cf. Hebrews 11:23. God always honours a mother's prayers.

Hannah

The story of Hannah and her son Samuel is one of the better known Bible family stories. Life was not easy for Hannah. To begin with, she found herself trapped as one of two women in a polygamous marriage situation. That in itself created all sorts of pressures, despite her husband's professed partiality for her. Added to that, Hannah was unable to have children. Distressing as this was in itself, her rival, Peninah, saw it as an opportunity to torment Hannah.

In spite of everything, Hannah maintained her faith in God and kept up her 'church attendance'. On one of her annual visits to the Tabernacle in Shiloh, she prayed for a son and covenanted with God that, if her prayer was answered, she would surrender that son to the Lord for the rest of his life. Although Eli, the spiritually obtuse priest on duty at the Temple that day, falsely accused Hannah of drunkenness, she remained confident God had heard her prayer. She went home happy, there to await the birth.

Hannah's deep faith and commitment to God are reflected not only in the naming of her son 'Samuel' – which means 'heard of God' – but in her dedication of him to God in fulfilment of her promise. Her practicality is seen in her regular provision of Samuel's hand-made clothing. She was evidently a capable seamstress and not afraid of work.

Hannah's prayer upon the birth of her son is one of the classic poems of Scripture and gives evidence of a deep experience of God, as well as a profound understanding of his Person and ways. This prayer may have inspired Mary's *Magnificat,* judging from its many parallel expressions and sentiments - cf. 1 Samuel 2:1-10 and Luke 1:46-55.

Eunice

The saying, "behind every successful man there is a good mother," is well illustrated in the story of this mother and son. Eunice was a Jewess married to a Greek (gentile) husband, living in the city of Lystra in Lycaonia (part of modern Turkey). She was the daughter of a woman named Lois, and mother of Paul's young friend, Timothy. We are not told when or how Eunice and her mother became Christians but it may well have been through the ministry of Paul and Barnabas when they visited Lystra on their first missionary journey c. A.D. 46.

Our singular lack of information about Timothy's father suggests he may never have trusted Christ, although, of course, that is conjecture. Timothy, described by Paul as "my true child in the faith", was a young man of sterling character and spiritual gift – cf. 1 & 2 Timothy. He joined Paul and Silas in their missionary endeavours, with the full backing of the churches at Lystra and Iconium.

From Paul's words in 2 Timothy, we discover that Eunice was a woman of sincere Christian faith who, even prior to her conversion to Christ, had valued the "sacred writings" - cf. 2 Timothy 1:5-6. Here are Paul's words as he introduces his famous statement about the inspiration of the Scriptures:

"But as for you, continue in what you have learned and have firmly believed, knowing from whom you learned it and how from childhood (*brephous*) you have been acquainted with the sacred writings, which are able to make you wise for salvation through faith in Christ Jesus." - 2 Timothy 3:14-15.

We learn several things from these words of Paul. The important one for our present study is that Eunice had brought her son up on the Bible. Sounds like the story of that other mother who said, "I brought my children up on two pieces of leather: the leather strap for correction and the leather-bound Bible for instruction!" That's a reasonable combination, even if 'politically incorrect' in today's undisciplined society!

Eunice, in keeping with well-established Jewish tradition, had helped Timothy learn his alphabet and first words from the Torah. This is borne out by Paul's use of the Greek word **brephous**, in the foregoing verse – it can mean either 'an unborn child,' as in Luke 1:41, 44; or a 'newborn babe', as here.

Timothy's character, as well as the quality of his life and service, is eloquent testimony to the effectiveness of this careful, consistent training, received at his mother's knee. Who knows what can be accomplished by men and women who are reared by godly mothers and brought up under the sound of the Scriptures? (cf. Acts 16:1-2; Philippians 2:19-23.)

Mary

Of all Bible mothers none was more privileged or more blessed than Mary the mother of Jesus. We have already considered her story under the heading: *Jesus and his earthly family*. However, no chapter about Bible mothers would be complete without reference to Mary.

One of the things that we are inclined to overlook in this lovely story is Mary's youth. While still in her teens, living quietly in the despised little town of Nazareth, Mary, through the marvellous ministration of the Holy Spirit, became the mother of the Saviour of the World. What a profound experience! Her unquestioning submission to the will of God, as well as her acceptance of all the cruel gossip she knew would surround her unusual pregnancy, attest to Mary's simple faith, determination and courage. Mary was no super-saint but a humble, village virgin who made herself available to God.

Like Hannah's song (1 Samuel 2), Mary's *Magnificat* displays a remarkable knowledge of the names and character of God. Her whole desire, as expressed in the opening words of the song, tell us how she revelled in divine grace and longed to glorify the Lord - (Luke 1:46-55).

As the story of her devoted motherhood unfolds, marked as it was by hard questions, unbearable sorrow, yet steady devotion, we learn that Mary's heart became a treasure trove of wondrous secrets.

Whether worshipping in Nazareth, traveling to Bethlehem, helping Elizabeth at *Ein Kerem*, serving at *Cana*, or standing under the shadow of the Cross, Jesus' mother remained true blue. Luke gives us a clue to her remarkable life in his final glimpse of Mary. She is on her knees in prayer, awaiting the fulfilment of God's promise and the advent of the Holy Spirit, coming to fill and empower his servants for world evangelism - (Acts 1:12-14).

Each of these Bible mothers offers a shining example for Christian mothers today. They show us that despite the challenges they faced, their lack of worldly influence and material possessions, they accepted their roles under God. They asked no greater privilege than this, to be faithful wives and devoted mothers. What greater blessing could we wish for our families today? Let us all - mothers, fathers, children or single adults - learn from these godly Bible women.

CHAPTER FOURTEEN

"It's Only Dad!"

We can measure the importance of fatherhood from the familiar, opening words of the prayer Jesus taught his disciples to pray: "Our *Father* in heaven..." - Matthew 6:9. Since God chooses to reveal himself as the pattern for fatherhood, that surely puts fathers on notice that they carry great responsibility in their earthly families. At the very least, it suggests that the *pater familias* is faced with two equally awesome tasks. On the one hand, he is to give his children moral and spiritual direction; on the other, he is called to model God's grace and care. We'll look at this in more detail when we consider Paul's prayer in Ephesians 3:14-15.

Fathers come in all shapes and sizes. Some are like tea bags - always getting in hot water! Some are like custard - they get upset over trifles (the English kind)! Some are like the keys to the family car - necessary but often missing. Some are like the family cat - they hate to be put out; while some are like Easter eggs - brittle outside but sweet inside. With some unfortunate exceptions, most dads are appreciated by their children.

Tragically, these days, many children have no idea who their dad is. It is unfortunate that delinquent dads often get more press than do responsible ones. No-one wields more influence for good than a father who cares enough for his children to spend time with them, to discipline them and to bring them up under the "discipline and instruction of the Lord." (Ephesians 6:4)

It is not easy being a dad nowadays; enemies lurk everywhere, ready to undermine parental authority. Christian standards are "honoured more in the breach than the observance" - to borrow a phrase from Shakespeare. Our contemporary society has lost its moral benchmarks. It is like a jeweller's shop after a 'smash and grab raid' – but with this big difference – the thieves are still in the store, changing all the price tags! By the time they are through, worthless things are marked up, while precious things are rated as dross. By many people, even respected teachers, God is politely bowed out of his world. Our children are exposed to all kinds of pernicious propaganda. However, be encouraged, Dad, for as Paul writes, "God's firm foundation stands, bearing this seal: 'The Lord knows those who are his.' " - 2 Timothy 2:19.

God's guidebook for fathers suggests three main areas of paternal responsibility. They are: instruction, correction and nurture - cf. Ephesians 6:1-4. We'll examine these matters again, in a later chapter. Of course, to instruct we must ourselves be informed, to correct we must ourselves be disciplined and to nurture we must be men of integrity. A father is called to make provision for the physical, intellectual, moral and spiritual development of his children. The words of the eighth century B.C. Prophet Micah seem a propos here, "He has told you, O man, what is good; and what does the Lord require of you but to do justice, and to love kindness, and to walk humbly with your God?" – Micah 6:8.

Be warned! If we fail to discipline and correct our children we are not only compounding present problems but storing up future trouble, both for them and for ourselves. The world doesn't need any more self-centred, ungrateful, disrespectful, disobedient, anti-social misfits – it already carries a full complement!

Christian nurture involves informing the mind, encouraging the heart and strengthening the will to practice biblical virtues. It is also wise to offer our children practical training: to show them how to use tools for home and garden. Such learned skills will be invaluable later in their lives. Certainly we must strike a balance. Paul warns against 'exasperating our children' – that is, being unduly overbearing and repressive. However, that does not mean turning a blind eye to wrong-doing or failing to teach and require obedience. (See Colossians 3:21.)

As fathers, we shall be wise to learn from our children, too. Surprise! Dads do not know everything, nor are they expected to be paragons of virtue. If we make a mistake we should admit it and say, "I'm sorry." Remember, it's quite okay for dads to say, "I love you," and to give their sons a hug – even when they're bigger than Dad! By the way, I understand – though I have no firsthand experience in this particular area – that daughters are also very close to their dads and need lots of understanding and affection.

It is a sad commentary on us dads that the Bible tells of very few exemplary fathers. Even the famous ones can teach us as much from their failures as from their successes. Of course, that can be encouraging in one way. It reminds us that all of us dads are sinners: only God's grace can remake us. By the way, our heavenly Father specialises in forgiveness. If, as fathers, we make the Word of God our guidebook, we shall not go far wrong. Always keep in mind that the God we worship not only reveals himself as Father, but cares for us, his children, more than we'll ever know.

Here is a little poem that I hope will encourage you as much as it has me:

> *A Father's Prayer for His Son*
> Lord God, who let your Baby Son
> Pass earthward where the joys are few;
> To a hard death when all was done,
> And very far away from you.

My little lad must go one day
Roads where I cannot guide his feet,
Through dangers that I cannot stay,
To griefs I cannot help him meet.

He must hear voices calling him –
When youth is wild and life is warm
And right seems far away and dim –
To evil things and battle storm.

Lord God whose Son went steadily
Down the hard road he had to tread,
Guard my son, too, that he may be
Strong in his hour of doubt and dread.
                                        Margaret Widdemer

Let me round off this chapter with a little story. Tom was fourteen and growing up fast. He couldn't imagine how his Dad knew so little about computers, texting, twittering and a lot of other cool things. However, Tom eventually finished his education and got a job. What now amazed him was how much his dad knew about the real issues of life, how to fix things and how to make ends meet. He asked his father one day, "Dad, how did you learn all this stuff?"

"Son," his dad replied, "I guess it must have been while helping your mum out and looking after you and the rest of the family!"

"Hey, thanks Dad, I love you and Mum," said Tom.

CHAPTER FIFTEEN

Grandma and Grandpa

Grandmothers are very special people – I am married to one, so I know! Of course, grandfathers are okay too! Like fathers and mothers, grandparents come in all shapes and sizes, and represent all kinds of traditions. They can play a very important role in a family. They represent another generation of the clan and give it a sense of history, stability and continuity. Grandparents usually keep family heirlooms, as well as fascinating photograph albums in which are pictures of their own parents as well as other relations. Incidentally, they have lots of pictures of their grandchildren's parents. These are not only lots of fun for grandchildren to see "how Mum and Dad looked when they were young" but can sometimes be useful if parents are giving you a bad time! Grandparents are live, visible links with the past and help to give children an awareness of their 'roots'. This is something crucial in today's mobile society where families move house on average every four years.

Some time ago I heard of a father who, as a matter of family policy, takes his children back to his homeland every so often, in order to introduce them to the village church he attended as a boy, and to show them the family gravestones in the churchyard. That may sound a bit macabre, but he believes it helps to give his own family unit an awareness of their history and heritage. My own sons occasionally remind me that whenever we visited England when they were young, I always took them to see the house where I was born and the little village school I attended! In retrospect, I have no regrets about that. In fact, nor have they, now that they themselves are dads – judging from where they take their children when they travel!

Grandparents not only serve as a mine of information about the past but can help preserve the best of family traditions. They also help keep the focus of a family after their own adult, married children have, for one reason or another, moved off in different directions. They tend to be the ones who keep in touch with everybody, circulate family news items and, most important, remember birthdays. Of course, if their family members still locate in the same general area, those frequent visits to 'Grandma's house', especially for dinner on Sunday, can be a great treat. She really knows how to bake the special 'stuff' grandchildren like to eat and she doesn't say, "It's your turn to wash up the dishes, Tommy!"

The younger family members are not the only ones to benefit from contact with grandparents. Having their grandchildren around them can give grandparents a fresh perspective on life. The children remind them of their own younger years and of times when they were perhaps struggling to bring up their own family. It helps them recall life's joys and trials and how they experienced God's faithfulness, care and provision. At least that's how it was in our family's experience.

Of course there's another side to this as well. Grandchildren can help you when you get stuck while working on your computer. They'll explain to you that 'blackberries' are not always put in pies, and 'twittering' is no longer 'strictly for the birds'. By the way, it sometimes helps if you are a little deaf since some of the 'music' your grandkids enjoy bears no relation to what you enjoy. If you use one, it's probably best to turn off your hearing aid occasionally!

Grandchildren can also be a great comfort when Grandma or Grandpa move on to Heaven. They help to fill the gap and keep us going. Young people keep older folk looking ahead, as they share their hopes and dreams. That is vital for grandparents who all too easily live in the past – as someone said, "letting their nostalgia become somebody else's neuralgia." Incidentally, grandchildren can wear you out so that even if you forget your pills and keep your teeth in, you still sleep better the night following their visit!

It is surprising how children, including teenagers, sometimes find better rapport with grandparents than with their own parents, at certain stages in life. Perhaps it is their availability and willingness to spend time that makes the difference. Or, is it that being 'in our second childhood' we relate to their situations better? Grandparents are somehow less threatening – they don't make the rules! Children will share their confidences more readily with them – and let out family secrets, by the way! This leads me to think of things grandparents should avoid or cultivate.

Things to avoid:
Try not to encourage the children to do things, when they are with you, that you know their parents do not allow at home.

Don't feed them things that may be nice but are not allowed, for good reason, by Mum and Dad. If you do, rest assured, you will hear about it later.

Difficult though it may sometimes be, don't spoil or indulge your grandchildren by giving them everything they ask for.

Be fair, try not to favour some of the grandchildren over others. You may be surprised, but the others will find out and so will their parents – then you really are in trouble!

Don't tell tales about your grandchildren's parents and, of course, keep confidences.

Don't encourage the children to regale you with details about private problems and happenings in their own home. That is not really fair and in any case you'll only hear one side of the story.

Things to cultivate:
Try to be available for your grandchildren whenever you can,

but remember that your energy level is not what it once was. As someone said, "You'll soon find out that your get up and go has got up and gone!"

Be ready to be firm and to say "no" sometimes.

Remember birthdays and try to give your grandchildren individual attention. There is no need to go overboard, spending a lot of money. A few pounds slipped inside a card will mean a lot. Remember you may end up with a dozen grandchildren before the party's over!

Encourage the grandchildren to practice good manners but try not to say things like: "When your mother was little, if she didn't eat her supper, she would be sent to her room." Or, "I cannot understand why your parents are not more firm with you."

Be sure to tell the children as much as you can recall about your family's past and take time to answer their questions.

Be good listeners and encourage your grandchildren to discover a living faith of their own. Of course you need to be aware of their parents' sensitivities in this area.

Express your love unconditionally: avoid bribes or threats.

If you find it necessary to discipline, make sure the grandchildren's parents are in agreement.

Above all, pray constantly for your grandchildren. They live in a dangerous world where so often the truth is denied: where decency and moral standards are ridiculed.

Well, the list could go on. As in most other relationships, sincerity and common sense are the keys.

A child's eye view of grandparents (How they see us!)

"Grandparents are mostly older than parents; sometimes they're really old. Usually they're lots of fun. If you're lucky, you get four, but most families don't have that many left. Every family should try to have at least one of each kind. Grandparents aren't as grown up as most adults, so they are quite happy to play with you – as long as the games are ones you can play sitting down. They have nothing to do, so they've got lots of time to tell you stories about what the world used to be like.

Chances are they'll call you by the wrong name, but that's okay because they even forget their own names sometimes.

It's better to go to their house in the morning because they have to take a nap in the afternoon, and they go to bed real early.

Grandparents know a lot about a lot of stuff, and they can do all sorts of neat tricks. Grandpa knows how to fix broken toys and Grandma is usually good at mending and sewing things. Generally, they don't play computer games and they think *iPods* are what peas come in. Some can actually take their teeth out at night, or remove their hair. Sometimes they'll ask you to help them find their glasses when they're already wearing them. Just tell them to look in the mirror. Another neat thing about grandparents is that they can tell you tales about your mum and dad. If you know you're going to get in trouble about some poor marks on your school report card, Granddad can probably find one of your dad's old report cards: that really helps! Usually you can only try that trick once! By the way, your dad is smarter than you think. He may even say, 'OK, bend over, I'll give you what my dad gave me when I got poor marks!' "

Does any of that sound familiar? If so, cheer up Grandpa and Grandma; just be grateful that you can still laugh about it. Remember, you are important links in the family chain. You will be a great blessing if you keep in mind the old motto: "It all depends on me, and I depend on God." Let Paul's words about 'trans-generational faith' encourage you. He writes,

"I thank God whom I serve, as did my ancestors,…as I remember you constantly in my prayers night and day….I am reminded of your sincere faith, a faith that dwelt first in your grandmother Lois and your mother Eunice and now, I am sure, dwells in you as well." - 2 Timothy 1:3-5

A Word to Seniors
Before leaving the subject of grand-parenting, it may be helpful to spare a thought for seniors in general. Obviously as

an octogenarian (or as a friend spells it, an 'octogeraniun'!) I have thought a little about this time of life. It is encouraging for Christian seniors to remember that the Bible is full of stories about older people who 'did exploits for God'.

Just think of Enoch who, if I read the story correctly, sired his son Methuselah at 65, then walked with God for another three hundred years - better late than never! Then there's the story of Abraham and Sarah, who despite their advanced years trusted God, and became the founders of the Hebrew nation. How can we forget the career of Moses, the man of God, who evidently heard and responded to the call of God at age eighty!

We can summarise Moses' life like this: He spent the first forty years of his life learning to be somebody, the next forty learning to be a nobody and the last forty years discovering that God was all he needed!

One of my favourites is Caleb, Joshua's friend who 'wholeheartedly followed the Lord.' Let's listen to his own words, "And now, behold, the Lord has kept me alive, just as he said, these forty-five years since the time that the Lord spoke this word to Moses…And now, behold, I am this day eighty-five years old. I am still as strong today as I was in the day that Moses sent me…So now give me this hill country ("this mountain" – KJV) of which the Lord spoke on that day…" –Joshua 14:10-12. What a challenge!! Granted, we may not be as 'full of vim and vigour' as Caleb, but we can, at least, count on God's promises, then seek to 'wholeheartedly follow the Lord'.

Of course we may choose to react like the rich old Barzillai. He turned down an invitation to accompany King David to Jerusalem because he said he was too old! This is how he put it: "How many years have I still to live, that I should go up with the king to Jerusalem? I am this day eighty years old…" cf. 2 Samuel 19:31-39. What a pity to miss out on such an opportunity. Barzillai's problem was that, like so many of us, he looked at his problems, instead of trusting the King to take care of him. So much for this brief sampling of Old Testament seniors.

As we consider our situation as older members of society, here are a few things worth keeping in mind:

1. Live gratefully and count your blessings – you won't have time to list all of them!

2. Accept your limitations and graciously accept help when offered.

3. Look after your health (without becoming a hypochondriac), listen to your doctor, take your pills and get your sleep.

4. Don't be constantly telling younger people that "hinges weren't like this when I was young" - just be glad a lot of them aren't!

5. Try not to monopolise every conversation, dispensing your unsolicited wisdom. Take time to listen – surprise! - you may learn something.

6. Eat regular meals and try to get some exercise.

7. Spend time with your family but don't overstay your welcome.

8. Give away what you don't really need. You can't take it with you.

9. Be sure to cultivate your spiritual life, be content, take time to pray, read the Word of God and enjoy the 'fellowship of saints'.

10. Get ready to go to Heaven. You'll be there a long time!

There's lots more, try writing out your own list. As you do so here are a couple of things to keep in mind.

Number one! - writing to a ninety year old friend who after a useful life in the Lord's service was now laid aside, Dr Billy Graham wrote, "W., old age is not for sissies!" How true!

Number two! - and this is rather more encouraging.

The Psalmist writes, "The righteous flourish like the palm tree and grow like a cedar in Lebanon. They are planted in the house of the Lord; they flourish in the courts of our God. They still bear fruit in old age; they are ever full of sap and green, to declare that the Lord is upright; he is my rock, and there is no unrighteousness in him." Psalm 92:12-15.

CHAPTER SIXTEEN

The Apostle Paul Talks to Families

Although not a parent himself, Paul's instructions for parents are both valuable and relevant, as the following statements show.

"Children, obey your parents in the Lord, for this is right. 'Honour your father and mother' (this is the first commandment with a promise), 'that it may go well with you and that you may live long in the land.' Fathers, do not provoke your children to anger, but bring them up in the discipline and instruction of the Lord." – Ephesians 6:1-4.

Paul encourages parents to be concerned about four things: obedience, nurture, admonition and love. Each is an essential ingredient in the Bible's recipe for domestic and family happiness. How sad, then, that many well-intentioned parents, even some Christian ones, neglect Paul's advice. Thinking they were being kind, by indulging their children's every whim, they discover too late that they have produced rebellious offspring. Not only have these 'spoilt kids' broken their parents' hearts, they have wrought havoc in the church and society in general. So let's take a look at Paul's four signposts.

OBEDIENCE

Scripture places strong emphasis on obedience to God and to parents. It follows that Christian parents should teach obedience and require it of their offspring. By learning to obey, our children can find out about social responsibility, respect for authority and, most important of all, submission to God. When parents fail to instil obedience in their children, both they and society pay a high price.

Paul very wisely inserts a balance in his teaching, both in Ephesians 6:4 and in Colossians 3:21. In the latter passage he writes: "Fathers, do not provoke your children, lest they become discouraged." We exasperate or embitter our children when we make rules and regulations without offering explanations. We can also do it by constantly nagging them or making idle threats.

Parents may lose their children's respect either by being too demanding or too easy-going. There is a happy medium in this, as in so many things in life. Absentee parents who are too busy to spend time with their children should not be surprised if their offspring are irresponsible and disobedient. Similarly, parents who are obsessed with 'ladder climbing' or with 'keeping up with the Joneses' may well find their offspring have already fallen off the bottom rung of the ladder!

It is worth noting that Paul addresses his words to fathers. Did he do this because it is the father's responsibility to lead the family? Or did he realise how much shorter tempered and less patient dads are inclined to be - when compared to mums? Probably for both reasons! Perhaps he had suffered irreparable harm at the hands of his own religious, Pharisee father, who may well have made unreasonable demands upon young Saul? We know he disinherited him later, because he could not tolerate his son's conversion to Jesus Messiah. There are still fathers around who seem to be more anxious to prove some minor point about their religious or denominational traditions, than winning their children for the Saviour. Christian integrity and gracious, personal conduct are more effective than sermons. Let us be warned: it is easy to win an argument but lose a friendship. Sad to relate, I know of too many people who would never darken the doors of a church due to the inconsistencies witnessed in their home, not to mention the legalistic demands they met in the church their parents took them to when they were growing up.

Christian fathers will better appreciate their duty if they remember Paul's point that God's fatherhood is their pattern or archetype. This is the gist of what he writes in Ephesians 3:14-15. Here are his words,

"For this reason I bow my knees before the Father, from whom every family (*patria*) in heaven and on earth is named."

Of course, such teaching is quite the reverse of contemporary, secular psychology which claims that our notion of God as Father is merely 'a projection of our innate father consciousness'.

Clearly, this Bible truth is as challenging as it is sensible. It reminds fathers that their children's idea of God is, in large measure, conditioned by what they see in their own earthly father. What a tragedy then, that the only concept some children have of God as Father, is the one they learn initially from a promiscuous, drunken, drop-out dad! Surely such men have a lot to answer for. As the strange proverb puts it: "The fathers have eaten sour grapes, and the children's teeth are set on edge." - Ezekiel 18:2.

Paul bases his call for filial obedience on four things:
- The Lordship of Christ
- Conventional family ethics
- The Decalogue
- The good pleasure of Christ.

The Lordship of Christ
Paul's qualifying phrase, "in the Lord," tells us right away where the focus of his thinking is to be found. He is talking about homes that are under the Lordship of Christ. It seems he is not just teaching general ethics but Christian ethics. We must ask some questions here.

1. Was Paul writing for the benefit of Christian children whose parents were not believers?

2. Was he reminding the children of Christian parents that their special privilege, as members of a Christian household, involved their obedience?

3. Was he advising children to obey, only insofar as their parents' commands did not conflict with God's? How does a Christian child, say, a teenager, respond should his parents require him to do something which he believes is contrary to Scripture? What if they forbid him to do what he believes is God's will – for example, get baptised? These are all challenging questions and might be included under the general heading "in the Lord."

Paul's reference to the Ten Commandments here, would seem to suggest that he was writing for the guidance of Christian parents and their children. He was saying that in a Christian home every decision and action should be governed by our faith in Christ. However, he was not requiring obedience only of Christian children. Children generally are capable of learning to obey from a very early age, just as they are of understanding the words, "Jesus loves me." Parents who themselves love the Lord Jesus and have surrendered their lives to him will find it easy to teach their children to obey. They are right to teach their children that obedience is required of them, if for no other reason than that they are members of a Christian family. This instruction applies to teenagers as it does to infants, although how it is applied will vary and require grace and parental skills.

Conventional Family Ethics

Paul's second ground for filial obedience is expressed in his phrase, "this is right (*dikaion*)." The word 'right' sometimes translated 'just' or 'righteous' includes the idea of 'conformity to a standard'. Paul based his argument for Christian conduct not only on Scripture – that is, 'supernatural revelation' - but also on instinctive or conventional morality. Most societies, Christian or otherwise, recognise the importance of children's obedience to parents and of parental responsibility toward their children.

Such conduct is regarded as 'right' in pagan as well as Christian societies. Most ethnic groups have their built-in code of family ethics, if only to preserve the culture of the group.

The Decalogue

Paul's third stated basis for requiring obedience is the fifth Commandment. This clearly shows the standard he has in mind. Coming from a Jewish home, Paul saw the universal validity of the moral principles of the Decalogue, as well as the benefits that accrue from it.

He writes, " 'Honour your father and mother' (this is the first commandment with a promise), 'that it may go well with you and that you may live long in the land.' " - (cf. Deuteronomy 5:16).

Paul, by noting the primacy of this commandment, was advising parents that they are God's representatives in the home. As such, they are to be obeyed. Paul's words remind us that while longevity may be a 'fringe benefit', any society that accepts God's Law as the basis for its family *mores* is likely to prosper. History confirms that when there is a breakdown of family life and order, there is a breakdown of society. Our present day social malaise, particularly in the West, offers striking confirmation of this.

Pleasing the Lord

In Colossians 3:20 Paul says that a child's obedience to his parents pleases the Lord. A child, especially one in a Christian home, will not find this too hard to understand. After all, the Lord Jesus was once a child, whose life in his home at Nazareth was a shining example of submission and obedience, cf. Luke 2:51. Let children be taught that when they obey their parents they are obeying the Saviour and making him happy. To refuse to obey is to reject both the precept and example of Jesus, which is serious indeed.

NURTURE

Parents are also required to "nurture" their children (KJV). This rather old fashioned word 'nurture' translates *paideta*, which is also rendered 'training', 'discipline', 'chastening', or 'instruction'. In this context it implies the active training of a child in Christian behaviour. Paul would, of course, remind us that it is important that we ourselves know what biblical standards of conduct are. His word, *kuriou,* ("of the Lord") - qualifies both *paideia* and *nouthesia.* Christian parents, while loving and appreciating them, should recognise that even their children (like themselves) have fallen, sinful natures. As one old preacher was heard to say as he held a new baby in his arms: "What a beautiful bundle of iniquity!" We have no record of the mother's response – just as well!

Paul nowhere advocates the harsh treatment of children, nor breaking a child's will, but rather helping to bend it through loving encouragement. Was he thinking of the words of the Psalm, "I will instruct you and teach you...Be not like a horse or a mule, without understanding, which must be curbed with bit and bridle..."? - Psalm 32:8, 9.

If the Psalmist's words are true of adults - and which of us would question that? - how much more so of children. His words teach us that the bit in a horse's mouth restrains it, while at the same time giving the animal the freedom and potential to be useful. Similarly, discipline helps a child discover patterns of authority, as well as acceptable behaviour.

"The nurture of the Lord" includes not only offering Christian guidelines but setting limits. Wise as he was, the Apostle understood that sensible young people, despite their sometimes vocal protestations, appreciate the freedom that *limits* provide. They will understand, and sooner or later be grateful for, honest Christian parents whose *nurture* is born of genuine concern and love. Obviously it takes great parental skill to impose guidelines, then gradually to relax control as children mature.

Although Paul himself suffered many physical beatings in the name of religion - 2 Corinthians 11:23, 25 - he nowhere supports cruelty to children nor to anyone else. People who see something sadistic or unkind in the biblical commands to use corporal punishment when needed have missed the point. Christian parents must be consistent, avoid emotional reactions, reject vindictiveness or resentment, and act wisely in love. There are all kinds of ways to discipline. Avoid the approach that says, "For that you can go and read the Bible for half an hour!" or, "Now you'll have to go to the prayer meeting!" Why should we associate such things with pain or unpleasantness?

INSTRUCTION

Paul's third requirement of parents is that they bring up their children in the "admonition" (*nouthesia*) of the Lord. His word has two roots, *nous* meaning 'mind', and *tithemi*, 'to place'. The idea therefore is to instruct or inform the mind. If 'nurture' has to do with action and example, 'admonition' has to do with sharing ideas and precepts.

The apostle's own Hebrew upbringing and training under the precepts of the Torah had convinced him of the importance of parents teaching their children about basic moral issues. Like Timothy, his son in the faith, Paul himself had known the "sacred writings" from infancy - 2 Timothy 3:15. It was this knowledge that had anchored him throughout his career. Writing from experience, Paul passed on this good advice to parents.

Like the "nurture," parental training was to be "of the Lord." Whatever else this phrase may mean, it includes the need for Christian parents to offer their children spiritual instruction and guidance. Children should be taught about God and the wonder of his great self-disclosure in the Incarnation. They should be encouraged to read, study and memorise the Scriptures. If this was important and necessary in Paul's day, how much more so in our dangerous times.

Parents must offer their children a clear understanding of the basis and application of Christian morality. They are wise parents who, like Lois and Eunice, share their faith in Christ with their children (2 Timothy 1:5). Parents who neglect Paul's advice or who delegate their children's spiritual training to others, run the risk of grief and heartache both for themselves and their children. The lax moral standards, the sexual promiscuity and the twisted propaganda of the contemporary media all conspire to destroy our children and our families. The careful and diligent Christian training of our children is the only antidote to counteract such poisons.

While verbal instruction is a part of this training, so is parental example. Christian morality is as much 'caught' as 'taught'. Lazy, unreliable, immodest, untruthful, discourteous, untidy, undisciplined parents are likely to rear children like themselves. There will be times when we make mistakes, but our children will accept them and still trust us, if they know that basically we are good and honest. In any case, there is nothing wrong with apologising to our family when we know we are wrong. We may lose face momentarily, but we will gain respect in the long run. Paul knew what he was talking about. Remember, he set such store by parental guidance that he disqualified from church leadership those who fail in this area, - cf. 1 Timothy 3:4, 5, 12; Titus 1:6.

LOVE

Paul urges Christian parents to *love* their children. Writing to Titus, he says that the Christian women were to "train the young women to love their husbands and children" (Titus 2:4). On the surface this sounds strange: surely a mother's love for her children is instinctive. But Paul knew his people well. Child abuse was common in the ancient world. In a society that worshipped physical strength and practiced flagrant immorality, children tended to be regarded either as objects of abuse or unproductive inconveniences. And so today, for all our vaunted sophistication, attitudes have not improved, in some circles. Witness the casual attitudes toward abortions, child pornography and the blatant abuse of so many children.

Paul encourages the early Christians to be different. "Let them," said Paul, in so many words, "show that they love and appreciate their children." His Jewish background and religious training with its regard for children as "a heritage from the Lord" (Psalm 127:3), is showing through again. Be that as it may, we must remember that one of the unique features of Christianity is the value it places on children and family. If Paul's words sound old-fashioned or strangely irrelevant to some modern, Christian parents, then let them consider the following truths. Nothing cements family relationships like parental love. Love is much more important than wealth, education, and all those status symbols so many parents crave for themselves and their children. Love is the catalyst without which nothing really happens in a family. There can be no true discipline where there is no love. Children whose parents give them everything but love are poor indeed. Those who are raised in a home where love is shown will grow up to be secure adults, better able to cope with the pressures of life.

How many unthinking parents, even some who are Christians, offer their children things, and 'bought pleasures', instead of giving of themselves and their time. Children need the care and loving support of their parents, not just 'pacifier handouts', and babysitters. The keys of your understanding heart are so much more important than the keys to the family car. Let's say it again, taking time to do things together may be demanding, especially for ambitious, acquisitive parents, but it will be rewarding in every way. Play it any way you want, the truth is, "The family that plays together, like the family that prays together, is the family that stays together." It is sad to see the way some families treat their homes like restaurants where they meet occasionally, to grab something to eat; or like dormitories where they finally get to sleep, at the end of activity crammed days.

Paul obviously saw the importance of the family and was inspired to write words that are still instructive and encouraging. Some of his critics dismiss his words as the outmoded advice of a fanatic, the counsels of a woman hater, or the words of a 'crusty old bachelor'. In so doing, they not only denigrate Paul but thoughtlessly rob themselves of blessing. For the Apostle, Christianity *begins at home*, and a great number of happy families agree.

Part 3

Contemporary Issues

"For I know the plans I have for you, declares the Lord, plans for welfare and not for evil, to give you a future and a hope. Then you will call upon me and come and pray to me, and I will hear you. You will seek me and find me, when you seek me with all your heart. I will be found by you, declares the Lord."

Jeremiah 29:11-14

CHAPTER SEVENTEEN

"Those Terrible, Terrific Teens"

Many parents dread the onset of the teen years. And, without question, this is a challenging time of life for everyone. However, it need not be so bad, as long as we observe a few guidelines and try to stay calm. We all go through the experience, either as parents or teens and most of us survive – believe it or not!

Adolescence is one of those important, formative, transition periods in life. It's a time of development and discovery. Changes are taking place physically, emotionally and spiritually. This calls for parental understanding, adjustments and love. We might also add, "the wisdom of Solomon, the patience of Job and the skin of a rhinoceros" – as one discerning person put it. Facing facts, being willing to learn and accepting advice from those who have 'trodden the pathway before us' can certainly facilitate things.

Physically

All kinds of physical changes take place as boys and girls arrive at the time of life we call 'puberty'. Generally it occurs earlier for girls than boys, but no matter when it comes it's a challenge. It is the changeover from childhood to adulthood; the time when a person becomes capable of procreation. Various visible changes take place and can, if not dealt with wisely, lead to all sorts of problems and embarrassments. In our promiscuous society apparently it is arriving earlier, so we all need to be alert.

Parents need to be specially sensitive at this time; willing to answer questions frankly and offer instruction. Sex education is best offered either by parents, by the family physician or by a trusted counsellor. Unfortunately, there are all kinds of other people who are anxious to provide their unsolicited help in this particular area. For a number or reasons such people are best avoided.

Psychologically

With the hormonal changes taking place at puberty come all kinds of mood swings and emotional roller coasters. While these are perfectly natural, they can be disturbing, not to mention disruptive. To be forewarned is to be forearmed. As young people develop their sense of personhood and independence, there will sometimes be expressions of rebellion, displays of resentment or a challenging of accepted family norms and authority. Surprising though it may sound, this is a teenager's way of asking for acceptance and recognition. Informed and aware adults will learn to cope with such behaviour. If we don't, once again, there are undesirables out there, waiting in the wings, whose solicitations are the very last thing our young folk need. What is more, the contemporary lifestyles and teaching of those who used to be trusted guides, such as teachers and counsellors, must often be viewed with suspicion, especially by Christian young people.

Spiritually

Generally speaking, most people reach the 'age of accountability' in their early teens. Judaism and certain Christian churches recognise this in their respective 'rites of passage' – take, for example, Bar Mitzvah and Confirmation. At this point in his or her life a young person is deemed to be personally responsible for the decisions made in life, particularly in spiritual matters. Of course, in many cases there are exceptions that prove the rule. For example, children reared in Christian – and presumably in other religious homes – may very well become aware of spiritual realities before age twelve.

It seems that with their newly discovered sense of independence, young people realise they are challenged to make up their own minds about the great issues of life. Many, who have made their decision to become Christians earlier in their lives, now experience a time of rededication or a deepening of their commitment. Some, sad to relate, realise that their early profession of faith was simply that, and lacked genuine commitment. As a result they turn their back on the Lord and go their own way, sometimes encouraged to do so by godless university professors and the like.

Parents and Christian leaders need to be aware of this time of development in the lives of their young people. They need to be particularly careful not to unthinkingly quash opinions which may seem to challenge their own long-held beliefs and traditions. Young people need space to doubt and to think things through. Certainly parents can tactfully help their teens find answers but we should keep in mind that personal decisions and discoveries last longer than packaged ones. Some second-hand things appreciate in value with time. That is not true of Christian faith. Remember, 'God has no grandchildren.'

Obviously, there is need for great patience and faith on the part of parents at this stage in a young person's life. A consistent Christian life, a heart open to God and a regular prayer life will not go unheeded. Count on God's promises and offer your teens all the love and understanding you can muster. Some things take time. I am reminded of the Texan who stopped to admire the large, plush, green lawn stretching out in front of an old English cathedral. "How do you get it to look that good; what's your trick?" he inquired of the gardener. "I'd sure like my lawn at home to look like that."

"Well, there's no trick sir, it's pretty straightforward," the gardener replied, "You just cut it and roll it for five hundred years." Enough said!

Yes, it's true; the best things in life do not develop overnight.

Parental preparation

Being prepared is half the battle. Quite frankly, it is too late to start dealing with the problems of adolescence once the teen years have arrived. Careful parental guidance, firm but kind discipline, patient, time-consuming training when our children are younger are the keys to coping with teenage years. Many parents wait too long and start too late. Sorry if that sounds like 'closing the barn door after the horse has bolted', but that's the truth.

Parents will be wise to seek and accept advice from Christian friends and families that have survived these years. Try to be understanding and open: you are not alone. There are all kinds of helpful books, written by professionals who are themselves Christian believers and who have had long experience of life. Remember too, that Jesus himself was once a teenager. As the story of his early life unfolds we see that while he was obedient and considerate of Mary and Joseph, he also asserted his independence - cf. Luke 2:49-52.

Some suggestions for parents of teens

Try not to overreact when your young people appear to be challenging your authority and your standards. Don't let it rankle when they do not readily accept your advice or when they appear to 'cut-out' on you. Recognise that despite their indifference, they are still longing for your love and acceptance. Don't be surprised if 'Mr Macho Teen' comes alongside his mum at the end of the day to enjoy a big hug! Of course, not all kids are the same, but then not every day is the same either.

Teenagers need to know that they are accepted by adults and appreciated for who they are. Unfortunately, for one reason or another – mostly the so-called 'generation gap' – many adults do not relate well to teens, and *vice versa*. As a result, a lot of teens seem alienated from adults. Parents in particular need to make sure that their young people are listened to and encouraged. Dad and Mum need to look out for signs of trouble and to take remedial action.

Teenagers who are into sport, or who are associated with a church, or who are working diligently at their school studies, rarely get in trouble. That should surely tell us something. By the same token, it is the 'loners', the 'introverts', and those who feel unappreciated by their family and other adults, who seek personal reinforcement through membership in gangs or other groups of social misfits. One of the tragedies of our day is the incidence of suicide among teens. The notes they leave often speak of loneliness, 'feeling different', or lack of acceptance by their peers.

It is never too soon to take time to relate to our children and to listen to them. On the other hand, it is often too late when rebellious attitudes and behaviour patterns have become hardened. This is not offered as a counsel of despair but as a wake-up call. Do not give up! Remember that dawn still comes around, even after the stormiest night. If problems have developed, then make up your mind to do something about them. Let your teenager know that while you may have failed in the past, you are determined to make changes. Even ask for their input.

Just recently I read the result of a survey about parenting in our part of Canada, which, incidentally, is notorious for its hedonistic secularism. Three quarters of the parents admitted that if they had their time over again, they would spend much more of it with their children. It has been professionally demonstrated that the best way to combat problems like drugs, teenage drinking, association with gangs and bad friendships is to invest time with our young people. We should also remember that our offspring learn as much from our own behaviour patterns and choices in life as from our instruction.

However you feel about their attitudes, tell your kids that you love them and appreciate them *for who they are*. As you go on praying, determine to be more available to help them with their struggles. Take time to explain why certain behaviour patterns and habits can be destructive. Try not to sound too judgmental. Believe me, there is nothing quite like the therapy of spending real time together. Listen, reassure and seek to share in some of the more positive things your young people like to do.

Do not be afraid to require obedience and establish guidelines. Teenagers, like children of any age, will appreciate knowing family boundaries and expectations. They may not approve, in fact, they may vocally disapprove, but that's all part of the game. The important thing is to communicate, give reasons and be reasonable. It will help if you remember your own teen years!

If your young people are Christians, it is helpful to discuss and seek to apply biblical standards, without, of course, being too preachy. If your family church is on its toes, it will offer helpful and supportive programs for your teenagers. If it doesn't, even after encouragement to do so, you may be well advised to find another church. By the way, do not be surprised if you find that your teens accept the wisdom and guidance of their youth leader or coach more readily than that offered by Mum or Dad. Try not to let it irk you, even if in your humble opinion the youth pastor is still 'wet behind the ears'. Hopefully he or she has been chosen wisely by the leadership of your church. In any event, he is much closer age-wise to the 'space' your teens are in.

Sometimes you will feel exasperated or even downright angry at some youthful escapades. Try not to lose your cool: avoid bad temper. Don't say things you do not really mean – wait till your blood pressure is closer to normal! Of course, if your house rules are deliberately and regularly flouted, there should be meaningful penalties. Rules without penalties are like a saw without teeth. Don't be afraid to be tough when it is necessary.

'Manners maketh man' – although that may sound like nonsense to your teens, stick with it. Today's secular youth are practically totally bereft of manners. Grunge, rudeness, insolence and indecency are the norms peddled by many contemporary, pagan teen idols. Despite that, courtesy is still a valued commodity in those parts of society that count. The home is the place to require and learn it. Of course, wearing sloppy clothes and dressing like the local farmer's scarecrow are not necessarily signs of teen decadence and need not be too loudly condemned. Teens have a tough time bucking peer fashions and pressures. Most teenagers wear a pout, ignore adults and wear their hats backwards – so what! As long as things are not too critical, evil or life-threatening, it's probably best to turn a blind eye.

Of course, parents will be wise to alert teens to the profligacy and blatant evil that pervades so much of the modern pop culture. Long, unkempt hair is one thing, addiction to the vile lyrics and mind-bending noise that masquerades under the name 'modern music' is quite another. Spiritually aware Christians will recognise good from evil.

Inform yourselves about drugs and substance abuse. Watch out for any tell-tale signs that your children may have been trapped into drug experimentation. Realise that drugs not only destroy mind and body, they open the door to demonism. It is no accident that when the Apostle Paul mentions 'sorcery' or 'witchcraft' in his "works of the flesh," the Greek word he uses is *pharmakeia* - (hence, 'pharmacy') - cf. Galatians 5:20. That certainly tells us something. Clearly, ours is not the first generation to be hoodwinked and enslaved by the "wiles of the devil."

If you suspect your teenager is using drugs then, without hesitation and against protestation, consult your family doctor or under extreme circumstances, solicit the help of the police. This terrible scourge is not something to be trifled with, nor excused for any reason whatsoever. Alcohol and tobacco are also addictive substances, destructive of body and mind. Purveyors of these items have unlimited resources to make their enslaving products look and sound appealing. They also know all about a teenager's desire to be 'cool'. Make sure you know who your teenager's friends are and with what kind of groups they are 'hanging out'.

These days, parents also need to be especially aware of the sort of things their young people are watching and with whom they are communicating on their computers. There is so much pornography and absolute filth on the web that people get hooked unwittingly, unless they are very careful. There are predators out there ready to seduce and take advantage of our children. Make sure you know what your kids are into. Of course the TV can be another subversive influence and that not only for teenagers! Encourage your teens to talk; let them know that it is because you love them that you want to guard and guide them. Be sure to underline the importance of staying in school and participating in healthy sports activities.

It is best to avoid belittling ridicule or biting sarcasm. Such things tend to dry up communication channels. Be quick to express your approval and appreciation whenever you can. Recognition and affirmation are particularly meaningful to a teenager. While we may be very aware of the many present-day problems of the teen culture, please be assured there are many terrific young people out there. They are hard-working, respectful and dedicated to good causes. They are concerned about the environment, ready to help people less fortunate than themselves and generally enthusiastic about life and true values. Let us do all that we can to encourage and boost such young people. Be sure to offer them a helping hand whenever we can.

Christian parents and teens alike, we all need to remind ourselves that we are simply sinners saved by God's grace. We constantly need to keep in mind the staggering price of our redemption and the wonder of forgiveness. Whether young or old, parents or children, let us stand together and guard our homes and families. Nehemiah offers us a good example. He certainly knew a thing or two about human nature and family values. Not only did he encourage his people to work together as families, close to their home, but he urged them to be armed and ready, and to put their trust in God - cf. Nehemiah 3:28-29 and 4:13-14. That's a plan that is hard to beat!

So be encouraged, parents. As God's children we have all kinds of resources available to us at every stage of life and family development.

To any teens who read these pages, let me say that even if some of us adults look as though we don't appreciate or understand your challenges and problems, we do! We admire your enthusiasm and your desire to change the world. In fact we wish we had half your energy, not to mention the opportunities facing you today. Be sure to take time out of your busy lives to read some good books, particularly Christian biographies. Get involved in a church and in some form of Christian service; perhaps even short term missions or helping in Christian camps. Such activities will inspire and focus your vision. Try to remember that you have lots of Christians praying for you. The Lord himself has great purposes of grace for you and will, if you let him, help you fulfil them. Finally, as said earlier, Jesus was once a teen. He understands your feelings and needs and loves to help.

CHAPTER EIGHTEEN

The Bible and the Single Person

Singleness, like single parenting, is such an emotive topic that we need to be sensitive in dealing with the many issues involved. The Bible recognises singleness and offers wise counsel, encouragement and hope. However, it nowhere requires those engaged in Christian service to remain celibate - just the opposite, in fact. Paul has some sharp words of warning regarding those who forbid people to marry – cf. 1 Timothy 4:1-3. Of course, a person may, for their own reasons, choose the single life in order to pursue some special service: that is an entirely different matter.

The Old Testament

The Old Testament has almost nothing to say on the subjects of celibacy or the single life. This is not surprising, since the Hebrews considered marriage and family to be regular social norms. Not to marry and not to have family were sometimes viewed as marks of divine displeasure. It would therefore certainly be hard to base a brief for celibacy, even for spiritual leaders, on the Old Testament. We see that the prophets - with the notable exception of Jeremiah and Daniel - the priests, the Levites, the kings, the judges, and all others who held office or were in leadership in Israel, were expected to marry and enjoy normal family life. That their marriages were sometimes less than ideal, and that their families were not always exemplary, cannot be denied.

However, despite the failures, celibacy was not recommended as an alternative. This still held true even when individuals took strict, religious vows to live the 'separate life'. Witness the cases of the Nazarites and the Rechabites (Numbers 6 and Jeremiah 35). The only conjugal limit on a priest was that he was not permitted to marry a divorcee, nor a prostitute - Leviticus 21:7. In the case of the High Priest he was also prohibited from marrying a widow – cf. Leviticus 21:13-14, Ezekiel 44:22. It was only with the development of community life, in groups like the Essene sect of the Jews, that celibacy came into vogue. Even the Essenes were divided on the issue; some undertook vows of celibacy, others did not. Marriage was practiced in the Qumran community despite its strong commitment to an austere, separatist lifestyle.

In one Old Testament story, some unmarried women were able to take their full place in society and receive the family inheritance - cf. Numbers 27:1-11. But even in this case, these women married later, within their own tribal group - cf. Numbers 36:1-12. There is also the rather unusual tale of Jephthah's daughter who, as a result of her father's rash vow, was never able to marry. In this instance we again see that the single state, far from being advocated, was considered less desirable. Perpetual virginity was to be lamented (Judges 11:38).

Our Lord's teaching

We have already recognised that while Jesus approved of marriage, he himself, like his forerunner John the Baptist, never married. His singleness was evidently necessary for the fulfilment of his unique, redeeming mission. Jesus touched on the subject of celibacy in his well-known teaching about marriage and divorce. Here are his words,

"Not everyone can receive this saying, but only those to whom it is given. For there are eunuchs who have been so from birth, and there are eunuchs who have been made eunuchs by men, and there are eunuchs who have made themselves eunuchs for the sake of the kingdom of heaven. Let the one who is able to receive this receive it." - Matthew 19:11-12.

To understand Jesus' words here we must see them in context. He had just answered the Pharisee's test question about 'grounds for divorce'. Jesus' answer was that marriage, having been instituted by God, must not be dissolved by man. His explanation about Moses granting a 'bill of divorcement' was really an aside from the main thrust of his reply. It was, in fact, our Lord's insistence on the permanence of marriage that occasioned his disciples' ill-advised comment, "If such is the case of a man with his wife, it is better not to marry." - v.10. One wonders if some of the disciples themselves were involved in unhappy marriages and secretly hoped Jesus might approve of their breaking off those relationships! If that was the case, then they were disappointed by Jesus' reply. Their words seem to convey the feeling that, if there is no way out of an unhappy marriage, then better not get married in the first place.

Bearing this in mind, we get the drift of Jesus' reply. He certainly repudiated all such negative attitudes toward marriage. He recognised that there were some people who were unable to marry because of congenital defects, or because they had been sterilised. But these were exceptional cases. Then there were others who had decided, for their own reasons, that they might better serve God by renouncing marriage.

Jesus, although single himself, rejected his disciples' view. When he said, "Let the one who is able to receive this receive it," (v.12), he was not saying that if a person can accept celibacy, he should. He was simply stating that a person should accept God's order in creation, which is 'one man for one woman'. To regard marriage as a biological expedient, or divorce as an easy option, would both have been unacceptable to Jesus. He recognised that such views represented a rejection of God's purpose in creating male and female as complementary partners. If this was difficult for disciples to accept in their day, it seems much harder for many to accept today. In fact, a lot of our contemporaries think of marriage as an outmoded tradition, and have adopted their own easy-going, divorce-on-demand, free love ethic. Hopefully, such aberrations would be totally rejected by Christian believers.

Paul's teaching

Paul's teaching on the single life is largely confined to 1 Corinthians 7. We see again that he favoured marriage and family life. Only under exceptional circumstances did he prefer the single state. Writing to the Corinthians, Paul did not, in fact, legislate either marriage or celibacy, but encouraged Christians to remain in the situation they found themselves in and there seek to glorify God – cf. 1 Corinthians 7:20.

Here are the Apostle's words: "I wish that all were as I myself am. But each has his own gift from God, one of one kind and one of another. To the unmarried and the widows I say that it is good for them to remain single as I am. But if they cannot exercise self-control, they should marry. For it is better to marry than to burn with passion." - 1 Corinthians 7:7-9.

At the time of writing, Paul was obviously unmarried. Whether he had been married, and his wife had died, or whether she had deserted him upon his becoming a Christian, we do not know – cf. 1 Corinthians 9:5. The point is that Paul, himself unattached, wished that those who were unmarried would remain so. Before looking into his reasons for this preference, we need to remember that the Apostle believed every Christian is responsible before the Lord for his or her own life and testimony. He recognised that some are gifted to remain single, while others are gifted to marry. Each must be fully persuaded in his own mind and not try to foist his opinions on others.

Paul's marriage ethic, here in 1 Corinthians, was predicated on the view, expressed in his phrase, "in view of the present distress," - v.26. Such was the situation in Corinth, and such was Paul's belief in the imminence of the Lord's Return, that he felt it would be better for single people to remain single. He recognised, as the saying has it that "he who marries and has children gives hostages to fortune." Paul's point in this context is that because of the very real possibility that some of his converts might face persecution or death for Christ's sake, it would be better for them to remain unmarried. He reasoned that it is hard enough to be tortured and cruelly done to death one's self, but to watch one's spouse or children suffer and die would be far worse (v.28).

Some of his critics suggest that Paul's phrase, "It is better to marry than to burn," represents a very low view of marriage, a kind of second-rate expedient. That this is a misreading of Paul is obvious not only from his words, read in their context, but from the high view of marriage he expresses in his letter to the Ephesians – cf. Ephesians 5.

The words, "it is better to marry than to burn," clearly relate to the specific circumstances of Paul's original readers. Living as they did, in the notoriously immoral city of Corinth, where prostitution was practiced in the name of religion, and where evil masqueraded as social virtue, life was a challenge for many of the Christians. So recently converted from paganism, some of them must have found the moral demands of the Gospel quite stringent. Then, on the other hand, there may well have been zealots in the Corinthian church who believed and taught that sex was a dirty word, even within the confines of marriage. Paul was realistic enough to understand these things, and obviously felt he must set things straight. He tells the Corinthian Christians, therefore, that there is more danger in repression than in expression. Given their environment, Paul recognised it would be dangerous for anyone with normal sexual desires to refrain from marrying just because he supposed celibacy was preferred in the Christian community. Paul was not offering 'counsels of perfection' for a spiritual elite, as some suggest, but giving sound advice to regular, Christian people. The Apostle was against unbridled lust and extramarital experimentation. What he was positively *for* was *marriage*, unless, of course, a person believed himself or herself called to the single life.

Paul makes a further point about the choice to remain single. He writes, "I want you to be free from anxieties. The unmarried man is anxious about the things of the Lord, how to please the Lord. But the married man is anxious about worldly things, how to please his wife, and his interests are divided. And the unmarried or betrothed woman is anxious about the things of the Lord, how to be holy in body and spirit. But the married woman is anxious about worldly things, how to please her husband. I say this for your own benefit, not to lay any restraint upon you, but to promote good order and to secure your undivided devotion to the Lord." – 1 Corinthians 7:32-35. The Apostle is anxious that Christians keep a right perspective on life and its values. He believed that the consummation of all things was near. Here are his words, "This is what I mean, brothers: the appointed time has grown very short." - v.29. He believed the Second Advent of Christ was imminent and wanted nothing to distract his readers, not even marriage.

Of course, it is still true that married Christians can be so occupied with the affairs of family life that they miss the purpose of their election by grace. That is not to say that single people cannot become just as obsessed with worldly ambition and self-interest as married ones. Each of us must decide on his or her values and priorities. For some people, married life and family responsibilities are great motivators for trusting the Lord. They can teach us how utterly dependent on God we are, not only for personal survival but for that of our loved ones.

So, while there is nothing intrinsically wrong with the single life, any thoughtful, honest person will admit that if one only has himself or herself to please, he or she is quite likely to do it! Conversely, if I am bound to consider other people and their happiness, I am less likely to end up like the 'self-made man who worships his maker'. Neither the married person, nor the unmarried person, nor the single parent, has any corner on devotion to Christ. The criterion of spirituality is not marital status but whether Jesus Christ is the Lord of my life and home.

Christendom's stated preference for celibacy over marriage, from the fourth century onward, not only represents a denial of Scripture but a rehash of pagan, Greek thought. The Incarnation forever refutes dualism's error, that, while the *spirit* is good, everything material, including the *body* with its natural appetites, is evil. It was that kind of confused thinking that led to the excesses of monasticism, asceticism, and the like. Fortunately, with the Reformation and its return to biblical thinking, marriage was seen in its true perspective.

Obviously, there is absolutely nothing wrong with *singleness.* What is more, if a Christian is single because he or she has chosen to be so, "for the sake of the kingdom of heaven," then we salute him. Others may be single, not by choice, but because the opportunity of marriage has not come. Any who find themselves in this situation, at least for the present, may see it as an opportunity to seek fulfilment by using their time and freedom to serve the Lord and assist individuals or families who are in need of help. Such singles should be encouraged when they remember that they stand in the noble company of such great people of faith as Jeremiah, Daniel, Hananiah, Mishael, Azariah, John the Baptist, Mary of Bethany, Martha, Dorcas, Phoebe and Paul.

Single Parents

Before we conclude this chapter, we must give consideration to those who are called to the difficult yet honourable task of being *single parents.* I have special sympathy for such, having been raised by a wonderful dad who, due to my mother's protracted illness and untimely death, single-handedly carried the burden of our home, while maintaining his work and faithful involvement in Christian service.

Single parents shoulder a heavy load and certainly deserve the understanding and help of their brothers and sisters in Christ. Some who carry such burdens become bitter and resentful and, unfortunately, even suspicious of those who offer help. It is better to face up to our need, seek God's grace to cope, and try to grow through the experience. How we face the challenge will determine not only our children's chance to make it in life, but our own wholeness in Christ. Of course, it goes without saying that the local church, as well as Christian families and individuals, need to be supportive of single-parent families, through our prayers and practical help. As mentioned before, I shall always be grateful for the Christian friends in our small village assembly who prayed for my dad and me, and helped us through some really tough times. My hope is that any singles or single parents who read these pages will understand they are not forgotten. Indeed, may they be greatly encouraged and blessed by the Lord!

CHAPTER NINETEEN

How Can Families Survive?

A lot of people are asking, "Can the family, as a relational unit, survive in our modern world, or is it another of the 'endangered species'? The answer depends very much on whose wisdom we accept or which signposts we follow. If we plump for secularism's dangerous stereotypes, then admittedly the family is in trouble.

If, on the other hand, we put our faith in God and obey his Word, there is hope. By the grace of God, not only will the family survive, it will prosper and continue to provide sound building blocks for a secure society.

Secularists tell us that the family is old-fashioned and outmoded. One American feminist, who scorns the traditional family model, oddly declared, "The Holy Family model of Jesus, Mary and Joseph is...an essentially repressive one, teaching authoritarian, psychological patterns and a belief in the unchanging rightness of male power." Fortunately, most sensible people will reject such nonsense. They know that a family based on biblical patterns and principles is still the best option for producing civilised people in an orderly, free society.

Let's face it - as Christians, we live in an alien world. For all their claims to be enlightened and liberated, many of today's popular gurus are themselves confused and afraid. They call licence, 'freedom'; perversion, 'normality'; and sadistic violence, 'art'. These so-called 'post-moderns' not only despise marriage and traditional family values but regard *in utero* children as expendable inconveniences. No wonder there are so many dysfunctional families, broken homes and abused children!

Without a doubt, there is a better way. As Christians, we believe that the family is a divine creation in which God is especially interested. He offers safe guidelines for its preservation – what we may call 'The Maker's Instructions'. In these final paragraphs we consider seven principles which, if adopted, will ensure family survival and success. We have alluded to some of these matters earlier but hopefully re-emphasising them here will help us remember to implement them.

1. Recognise the spiritual significance of the family
Not only is the family a creation of God, it is a revelation about him. When God created our first parents he said, "Let us make man (i.e. male and female) in our image, after our likeness." - Genesis 1:26-27. This suggests that our experiences of relationship and society are faint reflections of the fellowship enjoyed by God the Father, the Son and the Holy Spirit. Amazingly, this means that our families, with their diverse genders and personalities, can be a witness to the inscrutable mystery of the Godhead. The Fatherhood of God, the Sonship of Christ and the motherly 'brooding' of the Holy Spirit, as revealed in Scripture, confirm this understanding (cf. Genesis 1:2). We have seen that the Apostle Paul goes so far as to suggest that God's fatherhood is the archetype of all human fatherhood – Ephesians 3:14-15.

Scripture also portrays God's relationship with Israel and Christ's relationship with the Church under the figure of the marriage bond – cf. Isaiah 62:4, Hosea 2:16-20 and Ephesians 5:32. Obviously we must not read too much into this metaphor, but at least it suggests that our humanity and our families can teach us something about God himself.

Of course, the Incarnation was God's ultimate authenticating of the social unit we call 'family'. In this greatest of all miracles,

God in grace not only stooped to become one of us but entered a real human family. He came not as a forbidding super-man nor as a judge to condemn us, but as the sinless son of Mary, to redeem and save us.

2. Play it by God's rules

We suggested that the Bible contains the 'Maker's Instructions' for marriage and family life. How often when we buy a new gadget or appliance, we tear off the wrapper, then throw away the manufacturer's instructions with the box! Later, when the thing doesn't work, we get frustrated and wonder why our 'new toy' doesn't live up to our expectations. Unfortunately, at this point, we've not the faintest idea what to do about it. So it is with many families. They abandon the Bible, God's 'operating manual', then wonder why things go wrong.

While the Bible is not simply a book of rules and regulations, it does offer workable principles and guidelines which, if followed, guard against all sorts of dangers and make family life fulfilling. For example, Deuteronomy chapter six - so important in Hebrew thought - offers wise counsel about the place the Word of God should hold in home and family. Here are some of its 'sign-posts'.

"You shall love the Lord your God with all your heart and with all your soul and with all your might. And these words that I command you today shall be on your heart. You shall teach them diligently to your children, and shall talk of them when you sit in your house, and when you walk by the way, and when you lie down, and when you rise. You shall bind them as a sign on your hand, and they shall be as frontlets between your eyes. You shall write them on the doorposts of your house and on your gates." - Deuteronomy 6:5-9. Keep in mind, God not only offers counsel but grants the enabling grace of his Holy Spirit.

3. Practice consistent Christianity

It is James, the half-brother of Jesus, who challenges us about consistent Christian behaviour in his famous exhortation, 'practice what you preach' – James 2:14-17. Surely, if ever anyone observed a consistent life, it was James, as he shared that humble home in Nazareth with Jesus and the rest of the family.

Some people seem to think that because they get married in church, say 'grace' at mealtimes, tithe their money and do other religious things, theirs is a Christian home. However, as Moses' words in Deuteronomy indicate, there's more to it than that! We ourselves may make arbitrary distinctions between what is sacred and what is secular: the Bible does nothing of the kind. It views the whole of life as a sacred stewardship; an expression of our 'intelligent worship' – to use Paul's words - cf. Romans 12:1.

We shall be wise to bring every area of our family life under the Lordship of Christ - our decisions, our relationships and our actions. This will help us accept our roles and responsibilities happily, not grudgingly, however mundane they may be. Husbands will exercise their God-given calling to lead, in love. Wives will offer support and encouragement to their husbands. Parents will discipline and nurture their children with patience. Children will obey their parents "in the Lord." All will submit to Christ as Head – cf. Ephesians 5:21 – 6:4. In a home where Jesus Christ is Lord, there will be sacrificial love, trust, transparent honesty, considerateness, unselfish concern for others, and a willingness to forgive.

Let me share a little story about Christ's headship in the home. My wife and I spent the first year of our married life serving the Lord in Africa. One day we were invited to have lunch with a family in a little town called Livingstone, not far from the magnificent Victoria Falls. Due to his work schedule, the father of the family was not home. As our hostess showed us to the table, she asked if I would sit at the end, where Dad usually sat. As I took my place, I said, "Well this is an honour, to be the head of the house."

At this point, the five-year-old daughter sitting across the table piped up, "Oh, excuse me, but Christ is the Head of this house," then she pointed to the motto hanging on the wall. I was duly corrected – a little child shall lead them!

4. Accept responsible involvement

Fortunately, a family, unlike a chain, is stronger than its weakest link and is surprisingly resilient. There is an *esprit de corps* and a special ethos about a family which can be a great resource of strength and encouragement to individual members. However, only when each accepts his or her responsibility does the family function at its best.

A family is not so much a corporation as it is a co-op in which all participate, contribute and benefit. Children and young people should be trained to accept their share of household chores. The Bible reminds us that it is a good thing for a young person to face up to responsibility (Lamentations 3:27). There is likely to be much more involvement in the extended family than in the so-called 'nuclear family'. However, even where there is simply Father, Mother, Johnny and Mary, each one can play a vital role. There's no better family therapy – call it 'family glue' if you will – than total *participaxion* – to use a recently coined term. Whether it is a football game, a picnic, a holiday, or much more down-to-earth activities like cleaning the house or weeding the lawn, no one should be allowed to use the excuse of being "too busy!" And, of course, Mum should not be expected to carry the heavy end of the load while the rest get off scot-free.

Children grow up poor indeed, and handicapped practically, if they are not shown how to do things and allowed to do them. A son whose father teaches him simple plumbing or money management will always be grateful that Dad 'took the time'. A daughter, and certainly her future husband, will always be glad that Mum taught her how to cook. Parents do their children a disservice by waiting on them hand and foot, just as they do when they hire babysitters too often.

5. Cultivate a strong association with a local church

While Scripture teaches the primacy of the family, it usually views the family in the context of the believing community – the church. The local church, which is made up of families, relies on them for service and support. The strength of a Christian church is related not only to the spirituality of its members but to the strength and involvement of its families. Conversely, the family, as Martin Luther suggests, is "the school of the Christian life."

In our families we learn about rule, order, discipline, covenant, obedience and love. All these we bring to our church life. We have already seen how important the home, and our behaviour in it, is in relation to the church. Remember, the Scriptures make a man's acceptance of family responsibility one of the criteria of his eligibility for church leadership – cf. the Pastoral Epistles.

There are many ways in which Christian families can support their church. They will try to attend as many public services as possible, remembering that such attendance should not be allowed to impair the life of the family. A family can help its church through prayer, giving, witness in the community, respect for leaders, hospitality and sundry other services. Church families can stand together and help each other, especially in times of difficulty. Read how the Early Church members shared and helped each other.

The church has a special responsibility to care for single parent families, for unmarried singles, for people who have gone through a divorce, for orphans and children who must often function without any family support. Indeed, James calls this sort of thing 'true religion' - cf. James 1:27. For many people, the church can be like an extended family; a place where people who are lonely and alienated can find loving acceptance.

6. Make family togetherness a priority

Wasn't it Benjamin Franklin who said, "If we don't hang together, we'll all hang separately?" Sounds a little drastic but his point is well taken, especially by families. In these busy, modern times when each member of the family has a full slate of 'pressing commitments' – sometimes called 'the priority of the urgent' - it is easy to become hopelessly disconnected. We are all familiar with that very wise saying, "the family that prays together stays together." Well, there are other things we need to do together, such as, "eat together at the same table, at the same time, at least once a day!" Add to that 'talk together', 'play together', 'chill out together', 'have fun together', and so on. Our months and years together as a family under one roof pass all too quickly. Let them not be opportunities lost forever.

Beware lest, when our kids have done ice skating, skiing, soccer and spent their summers playing baseball and every imaginable community activity, we wake up to discover they have suddenly grown up and left for College or to get married! Sadly, in some cases, we've hardly had time to get to know each other. That may sound a bit extreme but unfortunately that's the sorry tale of too many modern families.

I saw a poignant strip cartoon recently; it went like this:
Panel #1 - Dad is watching TV when his 7-year-old bursts in with a math problem. "Dad, can you please help me with this question?"
"Not NOW!" Dad says.

Panel #2 - Dad is reading a review of the stock market when his son, now 11 years old, inquires, "Dad, wanna come and hit a few balls?"
"Not NOW, I'm busy!" Dad says.

Panel #3 - Dad is just leaving for a game of golf when his now 17-year-old yells, "Dad, I need you to give me a ride over town to pick up a book."
"Not NOW! I'm tee-ing off in ten minutes," replies Dad as, holding his clubs in one hand and his breakfast toast in the other, he rushes from the house.

Panel #4 - The son, now 20, has enlisted in the army and is leaving home.

"Bye, Dad," he calls.

"What's the hurry, son?" asks Dad, whose hair is now showing grey. "Can't we have a chat NOW, before you go?"

"Sorry, Dad, I don't have any time NOW. I've got a plane to catch!"

Well, enough said! Make sure that doesn't happen in your family, no matter how things may have been up to this point. Remember, time is a special gift we all share. As the little person asked, "Why is today called 'the present'?" Answer: "Because that's what it is – a GIFT from God!" You can use it, lose it, waste it or invest it. Family-together-time is an unbeatable investment that pays eternal dividends!

7. Renew your confidence in God

This is the number one key to family success. It reminds us that whether we are single or married, parents or children, we can only live responsibly and make our mark for God if we have complete confidence in him. While the New Testament speaks about Christian households, it nowhere suggests that becoming a Christian depends on our heredity or is guaranteed by our family connections. Unless we personally receive Jesus Christ to be our Lord and Saviour, our Christian heritage, like our parent's faith, may be as much a liability as an asset in the Day of Judgment.

Having trusted Christ for our personal salvation we had better learn to trust him for everything else. Remember, whatever we have, we simply hold as stewards for God. We must ever be aware of the danger of forgetting God when we become affluent. The wealthy family may be in greater danger than the poor one. Material things have ruined more homes and families than poverty has – not that there is any virtue in poverty! Listen to Agur's ancient prayer:

"Two things I ask of you; deny them not to me before I die: Remove far from me falsehood and lying; give me neither poverty nor riches; feed me with the food that is needful for me, lest I be full and deny you and say, "Who is the Lord?" or lest I be poor and steal and profane the name of my God." – Proverbs 30:7-9; see also Deuteronomy 6:10-12, 1 Timothy 6:9-11 & 17-18.

It is simply a matter of record that the more dependent we are on God, the more we shall draw on his resources and enjoy them. Children learn unforgettable lessons about God's grace and provision when they observe, first-hand, God meeting their family's needs. Christian parents would be well-advised to forgo financial and social ladder climbing. Better to set aside time to enjoy life's ordinary, simple pleasures with our children. Let us strike a positive note here. Trust God for our family life and for our children. When Paul answered the jailer's urgent question in the prison cell at Philippi, he said, "Believe in the Lord Jesus, and you will be saved, you and your household." - Acts 16:31. By the way, notice that the jailer's entire household *believed,* each for himself or herself and then got baptised in witness to their faith - v.33. Incidentally, there is clearly no support in this story for the practice of baptising infants, as is sometimes claimed by some Bible teachers.

What Paul meant is clear. On the one hand, salvation is intensely personal. On the other, parents may very well trust God to save their children, and faithfully pray to that end. In this matter, as in so many others, chances are, "[we] do not have, because [we] do not ask," or, we do not ask in faith - James 1:6-8, 4:2. Praise God for all who, like Timothy, can give thanks for generations of believing parents and forebears.

A story from our own family may encourage you to go on praying for yours. Mr. Ironside was a Scottish dairy farmer who lived in Aberdeenshire, back in the nineteenth century. By the way, the rather unpromising name of his farm was 'The Myre of Bedlam'. Every morning, after the early milking chores were done, Farmer Ironside would gather his family and farm workers around the breakfast table, read Scripture and pray for all of them including his own family "unto the third and fourth generation." God heard the prayers of that faithful man. His grandson became the famous Dr. Harry Ironside whose sermons and writings have blessed so many. We are grateful to say that our own grandchildren represent the seventh generation of Farmer Ironside's family! We keep a milk bottle from the Myre of Bedlam farm on a shelf in our dining room. It reminds us that God is faithful and 'has a very long arm'!

In signing off, let me encourage and assure you that God knows, loves and cares for you and your family: trust him! The stakes are high. The battle lines are drawn. The enemy is strong. His stratagems are devious. But we have God's promises as well as his abiding Presence.

Let Scripture have the last word:

"For though we walk in the flesh, we are not waging war according to the flesh. For the weapons of our warfare are not of the flesh but have divine power to destroy strongholds. We destroy arguments and every lofty opinion raised against the knowledge of God, and take every thought captive to obey Christ..." – 2 Corinthians 10:3-5.

APPENDICES:

Learning from Bible Families

Scriptures related to Marriage and Family

Suggestions for a Family Budget

APPENDIX ONE
Learning from Bible Families
(For personal or group study)

OLD TESTAMENT

	Family	Reference	Situation	Lessons, Observations, and Warnings
1	Noah, his wife, three sons and three daughters-in-law	Genesis 5-9	Lived in the corrupt antediluvian society	Trusted in God and expressed faith in action. Saved, blessed, and brought into covenant relationship with God. Family broken up due to the tragic effect of drunkenness.
2	Abraham, his wife Sarah, and son Isaac, his wife's maid Hagar, and her son Ishmael	Genesis 12-25	Called from paganism into a unique covenant relationship with God; Abraham known as "friend of God."	A husband and wife who rejected idolatry and materialism for a life of faith. Trusted God even in most trying circumstances. Willingly dedicated their child to God. Passed on a wonderful heritage to following generations. This story also warns against trying to do right things in the wrong way, and causing the family untold grief.
3	Lot, his wife, and two daughters	Genesis 12-19	A nomadic chief, nephew of Abraham; unfortunately had more money than sense.	A husband and wife who were prepared to compromise everything for wealth and prestige. Covetousness killed the mother. Drunkenness led the father to commit incest with his two daughters. Here is a striking warning to any family that puts gold before God.

Signposts For Happy Families

	Family	Reference	Situation	Lessons, Observations, and Warnings
4	Isaac and Rebekah and their sons, Esau and Jacob	Genesis 22-28	Abraham's famous son and daughter-in-law	A beautiful love story that ended sadly because once the couple married and became parents they showed favouritism in their family and refused to exercise godly discipline.
5	Jacob	Genesis 25-49	Founder of the twelve tribes of Israel. Grandson of Abraham and brother of Esau.	A large family in which every human characteristic seemed to be represented. Polygamy caused family strife and jealousy. Not much evidence of discipline or family feeling. Dishonesty evidently undermined family trust and loyalty.
6	Joseph, Asenath and sons, Manasseh and Ephraim	Genesis 37-50	The son of Jacob who became a ruler in Egypt	Although placed in a difficult situation, Joseph was a model of purity. An unfortunate family feud led ultimately to national division, showing how family problems can have wide repercussions.
7	Moses	Exodus 2	A family that triumphed over the problems created by slavery, racial oppression, and poverty.	Amram and Jochebed, Moses' parents, are models for all parents who would trust God for their families against great odds. Here was a mother who displayed great courage and risked everything to teach her children about God and the importance of true values in life.

	Family	Reference	Situation	Lessons, Observations, and Warnings
8	Joshua and his family	Joshua 24:15	The occasion of the renewing of the covenant at Shechem, subsequent to the conquest of Canaan.	Joshua and his household are examples to all who are willing to declare their family loyalty to God even if other so-called believers are vacillating. This family's motto has been a challenge and blessing to many ever since.
9	Samson and his parents	Judges 13	The time of the Judges, when the Philistines were attacking Israel.	Here are parents who, although believers themselves, failed to communicate their spiritual values and moral standards to their son. They appear to have been too indulgent and mistook spoiling for kindness.
10	Boaz, Ruth and Naomi	Ruth	A time of famine and recovery in the area of Bethlehem	This is the story of a family that experienced hard times and considerable misunderstanding. Despite the problems, they trusted in the Lord and became a blessing to the whole community. Here is an example of a particularly happy in-law relationship.
11	Hannah, Elkanah, and their son Samuel	1 Samuel 1	A time of spiritual apathy, if not of national anarchy	Here is a mother who, despite very difficult domestic circumstances which were aggravated by a polygamous husband, kept on praying. God not only answered her prayer and gave her a famous son, Samuel, but gave her strength and joy to cope. Her shining faith and commitment to God were a rebuke to the hollow sham of the religious pretenders around her.

Signposts For Happy Families

	Family	Reference	Situation	Lessons, Observations, and Warnings
12	Eli and sons	1 Samuel 1-2	Same situation as above.	Eli is a warning to all religious fathers, particularly ministers and church leaders who are so busy in their 'church' that they neglect their family. Although orthodox in faith and practice, here was a man who was spiritually backslidden and as a result helped his family on to ruin.
13	David and his family	1 & 2 Samuel	The early days of the monarchy in Israel.	Although famous for his feats and conquests, David was a poor father. His several marriages and strong passions brought grief on himself and his family. He failed to discipline his children and reaped a dreadful harvest.
14	The Shunammite	2 Kings 4	The period of the divided kingdom.	This is the story of a godly woman who practiced the art of hospitality. She appears to have had more spiritual discernment than her husband. When her only son was stricken she knew instinctively to turn to the Lord and cast her burden upon him.
15	Job's family	Job 1	This story takes place in the land of Uz, probably in patriarchal times.	Job is an example to all fathers. He not only spent time with his children but was deeply concerned for their spiritual well-being. He experienced terrible suffering and bereavement but kept his faith in God. He was one of the few men who could handle prosperity and adversity with equanimity.

	Family	Reference	Situation	Lessons, Observations, and Warnings
16	The Virtuous Woman and her family	Proverbs 31	A poem by King Lemuel, in praise of womanhood.	Here is an exemplary wife and mother. She is praised for her industry, wisdom, and careful speech. She supports her husband's decisions and regards domestic responsibilities and motherhood as a noble calling from the Lord.
17	Isaiah, his wife and sons	Isaiah 8	The scene is set in Jerusalem in the time of King Ahaz, eighth century B.C.	Isaiah, his wife, and sons are a living witness to the nation of Judah that God can be trusted. His children evidently stood with him and shared his faith in God in a time of spiritual apostasy.
18	Hosea, his wife and children	Hosea	Probably contemporary with Jeremiah, prophesied particularly to the Northern Kingdom.	Hosea experienced the special heartache of an unfaithful partner. Although his heart was broken and he carried the additional responsibilities falling on a single parent, he maintained his trust in God. His life was, in fact, an acted parable about God's unfailing love for a faithless nation.

NEW TESTAMENT

	Family	Reference	Situation	Lessons, Observations, and Warnings
19	Joseph, Mary, Jesus and his brothers and sisters	Matthew 1-2; Luke 1-2	The period of the Roman occupation of Palestine when the Herods ruled as vassal kings in Judah.	Here is the wonderful story of how God deigned to express himself in the context of a human family. Joseph and Mary are ordinary people who accepted the regular routines of daily work and family life. The story of Jesus' obedience and submission to Joseph and his mother, Mary, is an example to all young people. There were misunderstandings even in this family, but Jesus handled them without resentment. Clearly there was love in this family.
20	Zacharias, Elizabeth, and John	Luke 1	Palestine during the reign of the Roman Emperor Augustus. Zacharias and Elizabeth lived near Jerusalem where he served as a temple priest.	Here were two older parents who accepted their son as a gift from God. They prepared themselves for his birth and accepted the responsibility of bringing him up for God. Although evidently living in modest circumstances, they were content and made a mark for God.
21	Mary, Martha, and Lazarus	Luke 10:38-42; John 11	Lived in Bethany near Jerusalem and evidently owned a nice home there.	This is the story of a brother and his two sisters who lived very happily together despite their different temperaments. Given to hospitality, they often had the privilege of entertaining Jesus in their home. They had learned to bring their problems to Jesus.

	Family	Reference	Situation	Lessons, Observations, and Warnings
22	Mary and her son Mark	Acts 12:12-17	Lived in a comfortable home in Jerusalem in the time of the early church. Mary was probably from Cyprus originally and belonged to a priestly family.	Mary is an example to all women who have survived widowhood. She evidently busied herself in Christian work, made her home available to the Christians, and instructed her son in the ways of the Lord.
23	Priscilla and Aquila	Acts 18:2,26; Romans 16:3; 1 Corinthians 16:19	They lived during the reign of Claudius and traveled in business ventures to various cities of the day.	A husband and wife who exemplified the grace of hospitality. Apparently childless, they not only worked hard at their trade of tentmaking, but took time to help others whenever possible. They were evidently good Bible students and enjoyed discipling others.
24	Philemon and family	Philemon	Lived at Colosse, probably about the middle of the first century.	Although apparently well-to-do, they used their resources for the Lord. They were very hospitable and their home was the meeting place for the Christian church in Colosse. Paul felt quite at home with them.
25	Lois, Eunice and Timothy	Acts 16:1-2; 2 Timothy 1:5	Family lived at Ephesus during time of the early church.	This story stresses the importance of one generation communicating its faith to the next: Lois, a grandmother who prayed, and Eunice, a mother who taught her son the Scripture. We see here the great influence women can have by responsibly accepting and fulfilling their domestic and family responsibilities.

Signposts For Happy Families

	Family	Reference	Situation	Lessons, Observations, and Warnings
26	House of Onesiphorus	2 Timothy 1:16,17	Set in the city of Rome, probably A.D. 60	This family is an example to all who seek to relieve the difficulties and distress of others. They were exemplary in their courage and determination.

APPENDIX TWO
Scriptures related to Marriage and Family

1. MARRIAGE
Genesis 1:27; 2:18-25; 3:6, 7; 3:21; 4:19, 6:1; 12:1-20; 20:2-4;
24:4, 51-53, 57, 58, 67; 25:1; 26:7-11; 27:46; 28:1, 2; 29:18-30;
31:14; 34:12-14
Exodus 21:3, 4; 10; 22:16, 17
Leviticus 18:1-23; 21:13
Numbers 5:5-31
Deuteronomy 20:7; 24:1-4; 25:5-10
Ruth 4:5-10
1 Samuel 1:2
1 Kings 11:3-6
Proverbs 12:4; 18:22; 19:14
Isaiah 4:1; 62:4, 5
Hosea 1:2
Malachi 2:16
Matthew 1:24, 25; 2:13, 14, 20; 5:31, 32; 19:2-9; 22:23-30
Luke 16:18
John 2:1-11
Romans 7:1-3
1 Corinthians 7:2-5, 9, 10-17, 27, 39, 40; 9:5; 11:11, 12
2 Corinthians 6:14
Ephesians 5:22, 33
1 Timothy 3:2, 12; 4:1-3; 5:14
Titus 2:4, 5
Revelation 19:7, 8

2. LIMITS REGARDING MARRIAGE
Exodus 34:15, 16
Leviticus 18:1-23; 20:10-14; 20:20, 21
Judges 14:3
1 Kings 11:2
Ezra 9:1, 2; 10:18-44
Nehemiah 13:23-28
1 Corinthians 7

3. SEXUAL PURITY REQUIRED
Exodus 20:14; 22:19
Leviticus 20:14-20
Deuteronomy 5:18; 22:13-30; 27:20-23
Job 31:1
Matthew 5:27, 28; 19:18
John 8:1-11
1 Corinthians 5:1-5, 11
Galatians 5:19
1 Thessalonians 4:3

4. THE SINGLE LIFE
Psalm 68:6
Isaiah 54:4; 56:3-5
Jeremiah 16:2
Matthew 19:12
1 Corinthians 7:7, 8, 25, 26, 32, 34
Revelation 14:4

5. FAMILY
Genesis 1:28; 4:1; 9:1, 7; 12:1; 17:7-15; 18:19; 31:43; 33:2-5; 35:23-26
Exodus 12:3, 24-27; 13:14; 18:5
Leviticus 25:48, 49
Numbers 27:1-11; 36:1-9
Deuteronomy 21:10-21
Joshua 24:15
Ruth 4:5-10
1 Chronicles 20:8
Nehemiah 12:43
Job 1:1-5
Psalms 68:6; 113:9; 127:3-5; 128:3
Proverbs 13:22; 17:6
Isaiah 8:18
Matthew 10:34-37; 12:46-50; 13:55-57; 19:29; 21:28-31
Luke 1:5-7; 1:57-59; 15:21-32
John 19:25-27

Acts 16:30-34; 18:8; 23:16
Romans 16:7
1 Corinthians 1:16; 16:15
Galatians 4:1-7, 22, 23
Ephesians 5:22 – 6:4
1 Timothy 3:1-5, 8-12
2 Timothy 1:5
Philemon 1, 2
Hebrews 12:7-11

6. GENEALOGICAL TABLES
Genesis 4:16-22; 5:3-32; 10:1-32; 11:10-32; 22:20-24; 25:1-4, 12-16; 35:22-26; 36:1-43
Exodus 6:14-25
Numbers chs. 1 - 4; 26:1-65
Ruth 4:18-22
1 Chronicles chs. 1 - 9
Ezra 7:1-5; 8:1-14
Matthew 1:1-17
Luke 3:23-38

7. HUSBANDS
Psalm 128:3
Proverbs 5:15-19; 18:22
Ecclesiastes 9:9
1 Corinthians 7:1-4, 14-16; 11:3
Ephesians 5:23, 25, 28-33
Colossians 3:19
1 Timothy 3:1-12; 5:8
1 Peter 3:7

8. WIVES
Genesis 3:16
Esther 1:20
Psalm 128:3
Proverbs 12:4; 19:14; 31:10-28
1 Corinthians 7:3, 4; 11:3

Ephesians 5:22-24, 33
Colossians 3:18
1 Timothy 3:11; 5:14
Titus 2: 4, 5
Peter 3:1-6

9. PARENTS

Exodus 13:8, 14
Deuteronomy 4:9, 10; 6:7-9; 11:19, 20
Joshua 24:15
1 Kings 2:4
Psalm 78:3-8; 103:17, 18
Proverbs 22:6, 15; 23:13, 14
Isaiah 8:18; 54:13
Matthew 7:9-11; 18:3-5, 10; 19:14; 20:20, 21
1 Corinthians 7:14
Ephesians 6:4
Colossians 3:21
2 Timothy 3:15
Hebrews 12:7-11

10. CHILDREN

Genesis 4:1; 7:1, 13; 9:18; 17:19, 20; 21:1-6; 25:21-23; 27:25-29; 30:1; 31:16, 17; 37:3; 48:14-20
Exodus 2:1, 2; 11:5; 12:29; 13:1, 2; 21:22
Leviticus 12:1-8; 20:1, 2
Numbers 18:14-16
Deuteronomy 21:18-21
Joshua 4:21, 22; 24:15
1 Samuel 1:27, 28; 3:13
Matthew 18:2-6; 19:13-15
Luke 2:21–52; 9:47, 48
1 Corinthians 7:14
Galatians 4:19
Hebrews 12:5
1 John 3:1

11. CHILDREN'S RESPONSIBILITIES
Exodus 20:12; 21:15, 17
Leviticus 19:3
Deuteronomy 5:16; 27:16
Proverbs 1:8; 4:1; 6:20; 10:1; 13:1; 15:5; 23:22
Matthew 15:4-6; 19:19
Mark 7:9-13
Luke 2:51
Ephesians 6:1-3
Colossians 3:20
1 Timothy 5:4
Hebrews 12:7-11

APPENDIX THREE

Suggestions for a Family Budget

Note: A budget is only helpful if you:
A. Plan it realistically,
B. Stick with it and live within your means,
C. Keep it up to date, and,
D. Be sure everybody that matters is 'on the same page'.

Items to include:
1. Accommodation (Housing) – including: mortgage payments, rent, insurances, licences, taxes, repairs.

2. Utilities, including: Hydro – (heating, cooling, lighting, cooking.) Water, telephone, television fees; computer etc.

3. Maintenance: house repairs and décor, renovations, appliance repairs, garden, breakages and replacements.

4. Transportation: Car (include gas, repairs, licence, tyres, taxes, insurance). Replacement fund. Bus fares or other work and school travel.

5. Food and clothing

6. Medical costs: prescriptions and pharmacy items, hospital and doctor charges (or insurance coverage cost), dentist, other specialists and equipment.

7. School needs: books, supplies, meals, fees for extra-curricular items, uniforms, sportswear etc.

8. Life insurance, pension and professional fees, union dues, retirement plan, bank charges, accountant fees and legal fees.

9. Income tax (unless deducted with other costs at source).

10. Giving: church, missions, charities, birthday presents etc.

11. Vacation and fun money fund, eating out, family allowances and incidentals.

12. Miscellaneous and emergency fund.